SPECTACULAR FAILURES

BLITZ EDITIONS

Published by Blitz Editions
an imprint of Bookmart Ltd
Registered Number 2372865
Trading as Bookmart Ltd, Desford Road, Enderby
Leicester LE9 5AD

This book was produced
by Amazon Publishing Ltd

Cover design: Peter Dolton
Text design: Jim Reader
Production Manager: Sue Gray
Editorial Manager: Roz Williams

Printed in the Slovak Republic
51737

ISBN 1 85605 202 8

This material has previously appeared in *Fated Destiny*.

Every effort has been made to contact the copyright holders for the pictures.
In some cases they have been untraceable, for which we offer our apologies.
Thanks to the Hulton Deutsch Collection Ltd, who supplied most of them.
Pictures have been provided as follows: Hulton Deutsch Collection Limited (pp 2, 3, 7, 10, 11, 13, 16,
31 bottom, 37, 38, 45 bottom, 46, 47 top, 48 top, 51 bottom left, 52 bottom, 53 bottom, 55, 56 top, 59, 61,
62 bottom, 63–67, 69, 73, 77–79), Illustrated London News Picture Library (p 25),
Library of Congress (p 48 bottom), Peter Newark's Historical Pictures (pp 26, 27, 45 top, 60,
62 top, 68 bottom, 76), Peter Newark's Military Pictures (pp 8, 47 bottom, 49, 75),
Peter Newark's Western Americana (pp 5, 9, 12 bottom, 70), Popperfoto (pp 28, 31 top, 32, 35),
Portfolio (p 6), Rex Features (pp 29, 30, 34, 36, 39, 40, 41–43, 51 right, 54, 56 bottom, 57, 58 bottom),
Ian Drury (p 23), Syndication International Ltd (pp 12 top, 15, 17, 50, 52 top, 53 top, 58 top, 67 right,
68 top, 71, 72).

Cover: The main picture supplied by the Library of Congress.
Front left and right by the Hulton Deutsch Collection Ltd.
Front centre by Peter Newark's Historical Pictures.
Back cover picture supplied by the Hulton Deutsch Collection Ltd.

The Authors
Karen Farrington is a journalist who has worked for both national newspapers, and as a freelance, for the best
selling weekly women's magazines. Her broad experience has brought her into contact with some of the most
intriguing mysteries, compelling crimes and moving animal stories of recent times.

Nick Constable, also a journalist, has spent many years working in Fleet Street and covered top stories including
the famine of Ethiopia, the government-backed assassinations of street children in Brazil and the Gulf War.
He has also worked extensively to expose cruelty to animals in Britain and around the world.

SPECTACULAR FAILURES

GENERAL CUSTER
The last blunder

The ancient tribes, pushed to their limits by the land-hungry settlers, refused to surrender their holy lands. The arrogant General Custer was determined to make the Black Hills of Dakota run red with Indian blood.

George Armstrong Custer was a model soldier, the kind of man through whom wars are won and of whom legends are made. The legend of General Custer, however, is not one by which he would wish to be remembered.

Born on 5 December 1839 at New Rumley, Ohio, he graduated from the famed US Military Academy at West Point and was plummeted straight into the tragic American Civil War. He distinguished himself in this conflict by his pursuit of the Confederate Commander-in-Chief, General Robert E. Lee. By the age of only 23, he had rocketed to the rank of brigadier-general.

It was then that the vanity that eventually led him to an ignominious death first reared its arrogant head. He became a glory-seeker, desperate for mentions in dispatches. He grew his blond locks to shoulder length, and commissioned dozens of sketches and portraits of himself, with which he adorned his quarters.

His flamboyance and insufferable ego made him hated by his fellow officers, who were able to get their own back when, after the Civil War ended in 1865, he was relegated to the rank of captain. His driving ambition made him try all the harder, however, and he curried favour with senior officers until, within a year, he had regained the rank of lieutenant-colonel.

A LAUGHING STOCK

Custer was still a laughing stock among his peers. Perhaps it was one of them who reported him to his superiors for an offence that would have cost any other man his career. The long-haired egotist had found himself a wife, Libbie, and decided to spend a vacation with her – without troubling himself to seek permission from his senior officers. His absence from camp was discovered and Custer was hauled before a court martial. The sentence: suspension for a year without pay.

The delight back at camp must have been immense. It was the last anyone thought they would see or hear of the arrogant buffoon. In typical Custer style, he used his period of penury to write – about himself, of course! He portrayed himself in

Opposite: George Custer; the truth about his bungling was kept hidden for years.

Below: Indian chief Sitting Bull, who had 50 pieces of flesh carved from his body to prove his courage in the preparations for Custer's last stand.

the role of hero in a series of adventures that bore more relationship to fiction than fact. Unfortunately, it is these writings that perpetuated his image and restored his reputation. The truth, however, was that while writing his early memoirs, he was running up bills which, as he later moved from fort to fort, he never quite managed to pay off.

Custer's luck remained with him. In 1868 he was reinstated. Unbelievably, he was given the exalted rank of general and placed in charge of the illustrious 7th Cavalry. He was also given a special mission, one that required the virtues of a diplomat as much as those of a soldier.

General Philip Sheridan, nicknamed the 'Angry Bear' of the frontier forts, is best known for his pronouncement that 'the only good Indian is a dead one'. He is certainly not remembered for his diplomacy or compassion. Perhaps that is why he appointed the newly promoted General George Armstrong Custer, who also had none of these virtues, to solve one of America's thorniest problems. At the tender age of 28, Custer was ordered to bring to heel the ancient tribes of the Plains Indians.

THE WHITE MAN'S GREED

For decades, the Indians (mainly Cheyenne and Sioux) had been slowly pushed westwards by land-hungry settlers. Land treaties allowed the native Americans freedom of movement but in the 1860s the greed of the white man produced an increasing number of clashes between the new and old residents of the plains. Wandering bands of Indian buffalo-hunters were becoming an annoyance to the authorities – because they wanted the land on which the buffalo roamed. For these wholly commercial reasons, it was decided to push the Indians into reservations. Many refused, preferring a precarious existence on the plains to mere survival on reservation handouts. The government wanted 'these renegades, these outcasts, these anti-socials' to be made to see the error of their ancient ways.

Why Custer should have been chosen as the man to get this message across can only be a matter of conjecture. His career as a soldier had been extremely patchy, and he

was desperate to rehabilitate himself with the senior staff. He needed success and yearned for glory. It must have been made clear to him by General Sheridan that a handful of despised Indians must not be allowed to stand in his way.

In fact, Custer's mission was: 'To proceed to Washita River, the winter seat of the hostile tribes, and then to destroy their villages and ponies, kill or hang all warriors and bring back all women and children'.

The general was delighted to accept the task. In the autumn of 1868, he rode out towards the west, revelling in the nicknames the Indians had given him – 'Hard Backsides' because of the long chases he made without leaving the saddle, and the 'Long-Haired One' (or *Pahuska*) because of his flowing, straw-coloured locks.

His first foe was to be a peaceable old chief called Black Kettle, leader of the Southern Cheyenne, who had settled with his tribe of 200 families on the bank of the Washita River – the same river mentioned in Custer's secret orders.

Winter was about to set in and Black Kettle had asked to be allowed to move his tribe to the protection of the nearest white military outpost, Fort Cobb, about 100 miles distant. General William Hazen, the fort's commander, had refused, ordering Black Kettle and his deputation to return to the Washita. The general had, however, given them a firm assurance of safety. He had promised them that they would be allowed to remain by the river until after the snows had melted.

Did General Hazen know he was lying? Or did General Custer decide to overrule him? All that is certain is that before dawn on a foggy December morning, Custer's men surrounded the Cheyenne camp. Puzzled, Black Kettle saddled up and rode out through the mist to find the leader of the whites and talk with him.

SLAUGHTER OF INNOCENTS

As the Cheyenne chief left his camp, the cavalry charged. According to Indian legend, he was shot dead as he raised his hand to greet the approaching soldiers.

A massacre followed. Custer's secret orders were to kill the warriors, but it is estimated that only ten of the victims were warriors. The other 100 were men, young and old, women and children executed indiscriminately. Another 50 women and children were taken prisoner as a warning against retaliation. As a final blow, hundreds of ponies were slaughtered so that the survivors would have no means of flight.

This act of ignominy was but the first of a series of merciless campaigns throughout the winter against all other Indians in the area. Custer encouraged the reputation of himself as a pitiless warrior against whom no Indian dare stand. For a while, he succeeded. Then he met his match – in the Sioux chief Sitting Bull.

The word 'Sioux' is an alternative to Dakota, and in 1868 the Black Hills of Dakota had been given for all time to the Indians who lived there. This treaty suited the white man because the hills were thought valueless. But in 1874 Custer led an expedition into the region and reported: 'The hills are full of gold from the grass roots down.' The local military authorities tried to renegotiate a treaty but the Indians would not budge. Their hills, the 'Paha Sapa', were holy places, the centre of their spirit world, and they would not give them up.

A commission was sent from Washington to meet not only the Sioux but also the Arapahos and Cheyenne, all of whom had claims to the Black Hills. The tribes were unwilling to sell their land or to exchange it for other territory. Sitting Bull warned: 'We want to sell none of our land – not even a pinch of dust. The Black Hills belong to us. We want no white men here. If the white man tries to take the hills, we will fight.'

The reaction of the white man was predictable. The treaty was torn up and Custer pushed a trail through to open up the wealth of the Black Hills. In the Sioux language it was known as the 'Thieves Road'. The War Department leapt into action, issuing a hypocritical ultimatum that any Indians not on their official reservations by the end of January 1876 would be considered hostile and that 'military force will be sent to compel them'.

At this, Sitting Bull proved himself a better diplomat than the commissioners or the War Department. He protested in the

most measured terms that he had received news of the ultimatum only three weeks before the deadline. It would be impossible for his tribe to move camp in midwinter. The government was confounded. Genocide could not be sanctioned, and there was no good excuse to implement such a policy.

Instead of acting openly, the War Department resorted to subterfuge and deceit. On 7 February they ordered General Sheridan to attack the Indians. He entrusted the task to his fiercest commander, General George Armstrong Custer.

This was to be Custer's greatest hour. He left the safety of Fort Abraham Lincoln, in North Dakota, and journeyed westward. Every night of his journey, he sent a dispatch to New York newspapers, relating tales of his own courage and imagination. He also kept a 'private' diary – which he meant to be published later for his own self-glorification. In it he wrote: 'In years long-numbered with the past, my every thought was ambitious. Not to be wealthy,

Above: *One of Custer's scouts, Curley, a member of the Crow tribe. He was one of the few to survive the massacre at Little Big Horn though his life was not spared out of any racial loyalty. Sitting Bull's warriors were too busy slaughtering white men.*

THE GREEDY WHITE MEN THOUGHT THE HILLS WERE FULL OF GOLD AND WERE HAPPY TO MASSACRE INDIAN WOMEN AND CHILDREN TO GET THEIR HANDS ON IT.

Above: The *Battle of Little Bighorn, 1876*.

not to be learned, but to be great. I desired to link my name with acts and men, and in such a manner as to be a mark of honour, not only to the present, but to future generations.'

The campaign against the tribes settled around the Montana–Wyoming border began slowly. Cavalry would attack an isolated Indian encampment and burn its tepees. Often they would shoot the horses. Feeling increasingly isolated, the scattered Indians began to band together for safety in the Powder River and Tongue River basins. Eventually, a 'mega-tribe' came into being, comprising at least 10,000 Indians, of whom some 3,000 or 4,000 were warriors. They lived in a veritable forest of tepees and makeshift tents stretching three miles along the west bank of the Little Bighorn River. The Indians termed the camp the 'Valley of the Greasy Grass'. The whites knew the area as simply 'Little Bighorn'.

A GREAT POWER

Here were gathered the Hunkpapas, as well as Blackfoot Sioux, Arapahos, Sans Arcs, Brules, Minneconjous and Cheyenne. But the camp's leader was the Hunkpapa chief Sitting Bull, of whom a cavalry scout named Lewis Dewitt left us this description:

'Sitting Bull had a great power over the Sioux. He knew how to lead them. He told the Sioux many times that he was not made to be a reservation Indian. The Great Spirit had made him free to go wherever he wished, to hunt buffalo and to be a leader of his tribe.'

By June 1876, they all knew that a great battle was imminent. The Sioux feasted on buffalo meat, danced and chanted around their fires. Sitting Bull had 50 pieces of flesh cut from his body to prove his courage. Then he went into a trance. When he was revived, he told the tribe that he had seen a wonderful vision. He had seen white soldiers 'falling like grasshoppers' into his camp while a voice said: 'I give you these because they have no ears.'

On the night of 24 June 1876, while the Sioux held a holy sun dance to strengthen their resolve for battle and to ensure that the spirits of their dead would fly heavenward, General Custer arrived at the valley of the Little Bighorn. In his desperation for battle, he had outstripped his other units (he had made 60 miles in just two days) and turned up across the river from Sitting Bull's camp with 12 troops of US Cavalry – just 611 men.

Other detachments were on the way. Major-General John Gibbon had marched east from Fort Ellis, and General Alfred Terry had marched west from Fort Abraham Lincoln to meet up with him on the Yellowstone River. The two were now moving up the Little Bighorn with their combined force of 1,500 men.

Another 1,000 soldiers, led by General George Crook, straggled far to the south on the journey from Fort Fetterman. They were slightly less anxious for battle, already having encountered a war party of Oglalas, led by their fearsome chief Crazy Horse. The Oglalas had made a daring sortie to ambush Crook's men in the valley of the River Rosebud. Indeed, they almost succeeded in wiping out the force, such was the hopeless leadership of the general. He was saved, however, by the bravery of a party of Indian allies he had brought along as mercenaries: 250 Sioux-hating Crows and Shoshonis.

Custer was unaware that Crook was delayed and that his force was in total disarray. He knew that his other fellow generals were on their way, however, and was anxious that they should not share the glory of victory.

Now knowing the size of the Indian camp, Custer should have been concerned at his tactical disadvantage. He also should have reviewed his decision to turn down General Terry's offer of extra men and Gatling guns, which he believed would have held up his progress. And he certainly should have heeded his own Indian scouts, who begged him to hold back for two days until Terry and Gibbon caught up with them.

But General Custer was too arrogant to heed any such advice. He was too vainglorious to delay attacking Sitting Bull for one day longer …

At dawn on 25 June, Custer launched his attack. He advanced with three of his 12 troops, while another three moved forward under Captain Frederick Benteen and a further three under Major Marcus Reno. The remaining troops were left with the supply train.

Major Reno's modest force of 140 men crossed the Little Bighorn River and successfully attacked from the rear, taking by surprise the Hunkpapas, Blackfoot Sioux and Crazy Horse's Oglalas in their villages at the southern end of the camp. Women and children were cruelly shot down as they ventured from their tepees.

At the moment of Reno's attack, Custer and his much larger force of 225 men were scheduled to be attacking the Indians from the other side. But Custer was still four miles away – stumbling along the river bank looking for a suitable crossing. Likewise, the third column, under Captain Benteen, was still some miles from its target.

A GOOD DAY TO DIE

Reno could not sustain the attack alone. Sitting Bull's chief lieutenant, Gall, who had just seen his wife and children cut down by the troops, rallied his warriors for a counter-attack. Out-flanked,

TERRIFIED WOMEN AND CHILDREN WERE COLD-BLOODEDLY SHOT TO PIECES AS THEY SOUGHT SANCTUARY.

Below: *Custer's last stand, from an engraving. Even though the defeat was brought about by his hasty pursuit of glory, he was still seen as a hero.*

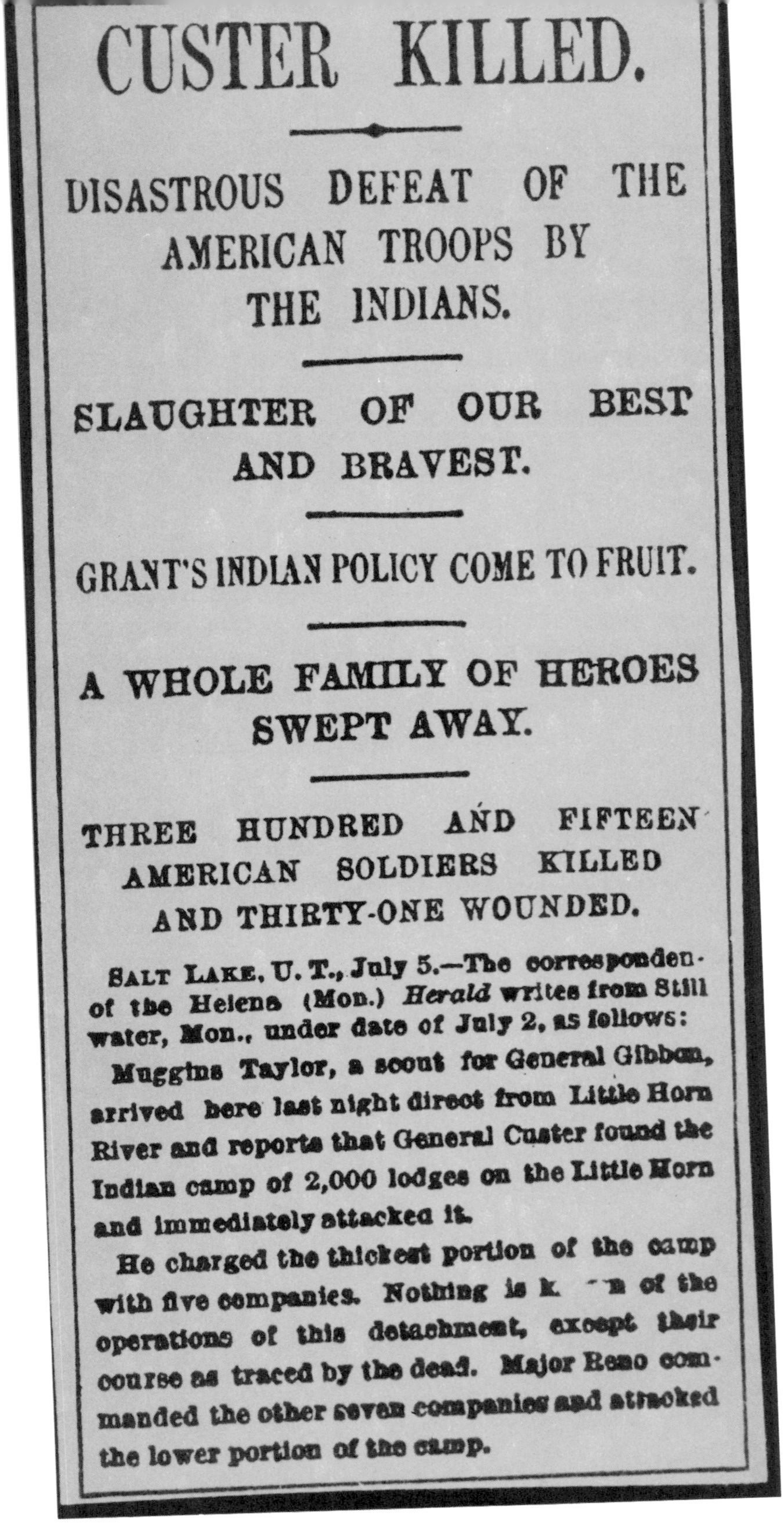

CUSTER KILLED.

DISASTROUS DEFEAT OF THE AMERICAN TROOPS BY THE INDIANS.

SLAUGHTER OF OUR BEST AND BRAVEST.

GRANT'S INDIAN POLICY COME TO FRUIT.

A WHOLE FAMILY OF HEROES SWEPT AWAY.

THREE HUNDRED AND FIFTEEN AMERICAN SOLDIERS KILLED AND THIRTY-ONE WOUNDED.

SALT LAKE, U. T., July 5.—The correspondent of the Helena (Mon.) Herald writes from Still water, Mon., under date of July 2, as follows:

Muggins Taylor, a scout for General Gibbon, arrived here last night direct from Little Horn River and reports that General Custer found the Indian camp of 2,000 lodges on the Little Horn and immediately attacked it.

He charged the thickest portion of the camp with five companies. Nothing is k — n of the operations of this detachment, except their course as traced by the dead. Major Reno commanded the other seven companies and attacked the lower portion of the camp.

Above: New York World *told how the Indians had massacred 'hero' soldiers. The report appeared on 6 July 1876.*

outnumbered, and exhausted from their forced march, Reno's men retreated.

The vengeful Crazy Horse told his men: '*Hoka-hey!* It's a good day to fight. It's a good day to die. Strong hearts, brave hearts to the front, weak hearts and cowards to the rear.'

Now Sitting Bull, directing the battle from the high ground of his tepee, could vent his wrath against the hated *Pahuska* …

He ordered his chief lieutenant, the ferocious Gall, to ford the river to the rear of Custer's force and to take it from behind. The general was taken completely by surprise. In panic, he ordered his men to retreat to a nearby hill and take up defensive positions.

Struggling up this rise, with Gall's men screaming for blood at their heels, General George Custer must at last have lost his arrogant smirk. For there, atop the hill and staring down at him was Crazy Horse – with 1,000 mounted warriors. Custer was at a loss for words. He could not voice his next command. His troops were terrified. There was nowhere to run. Their leader, the 'Long-Haired One', was not invincible. He was suddenly proved to be one of history's biggest bunglers.

The force of 225 that Custer had led to war with the promise of victory and glory now stared death in the face. Crazy Horse's men delayed their revenge for a few moments as they stared down in disdain at the cowering cavalry. Then they charged.

The soldiers dismounted. Without a shred of cover, they grouped themselves in a broad circle and set about defending themselves with the resigned bravery of lost men. Whooping and shouting and screaming, the shrieking Sioux shot away at the cavalrymen. They fell by the score until a remaining few at the edge of the battle held up their hands in surrender. They were immediately hacked to death.

But where, Crazy Horse demanded, was *Pahuska*? Suddenly, Custer stood alone – in Sitting Bull's words, 'like a sheaf of corn with all the ears fallen around him'. He had been unrecognized at first because he had had his long hair cut short for the battle. But now they knew him, the Indians descended on him like flies to carrion.

Sitting Bull, Crazy Horse and their men celebrated their victory and mourned their dead. They had defended their people and their land with determination and valour. But in Washington Custer's Last Stand was labelled a savage massacre.

The body of the incompetent, arrogant, vanquished General Custer was recovered and given a hero's burial at West Point. Meanwhile, a series of punitive missions was launched against the victorious Indians, who quickly scattered.

Sitting Bull fled with 3,000 warriors to Canada, the 'Land of the Great Godmother', Queen Victoria. In 1881 he returned to the US and surrendered, spending two years in prison before being allowed to rejoin his tribe at Standing Rock reservation, North Dakota. Nine years later he was accused of once again inciting unrest among his people. Resisting arrest, he was shot in the back.

Crazy Horse also surrendered and moved to a reservation. But in 1877 he was taken to Fort Robinson where, while trying to escape, he was bayoneted to death. His last words were: 'Let me go, my friends. You have got me hurt enough.'

Custer, on the other hand, remained a hero. His phony legend of heroism took a century to dispel. The blindly blundering story of the man who by treachery and butchery helped wipe out entire nations has only recently been told.

Above: *Following the battle, Americans come to pay their respects at the graves of the men who died.*

Left: *Fearsome Oglala leader Crazy Horse. After Indian women and children were brutally murdered by the cavalry, he showed no mercy at Little Bighorn.*

CHRISTOPHER COLUMBUS Who really discovered America?

Columbus was determined to sail to the ends of the Earth in search of the riches of the Orient. Instead he stumbled across America, firmly believing that the West was really the East ...

Ask any schoolchild: 'Who discovered America?' and the answer is likely to come straight back: 'Christopher Columbus'. But should the great navigator really get the credit for being the first man to open up the New World to the Old? Or did the Chinese, Phoenician, Irish, Viking or Ancient Greek sailors get there first? And, to rewrite history even further, did Columbus really mean to discover America? Was not his voyage one of the most enduring errors in history?

Christopher Columbus was without doubt the most pioneering voyager of his age, a brave and ambitious sailor who discovered America in 1492 when he traversed the unknown Atlantic from Spain to the West Indies. Generations of schoolchildren have grown up believing the great navigator opened up this Brave New World.

What they have not been taught is the astonishing catalogue of errors that led to his remarkable ocean voyages ...

Christopher Columbus was born Cristoforo Columbo, son of a clothmaker in Genoa, Italy, in about 1451. Little is known of his early life, but he went to sea as a youth and joined the Portuguese fleet after being shipwrecked off Lisbon in 1476.

A DREAM OF RICHES

A proud, stubborn, ambitious mariner, he was convinced the world was round – an unpopular theory in his day, but one that was gaining support among the scientific brains of Europe. He believed that the coast of spice-rich Asia and the gold-rich lands of the Orient lay west of Europe, and he dreamed of opening up a new sea route from Spain to the isles of the East Indies.

Ironically, many of the theories which were to lead Columbus to the New World were based on fallacy and wholly misinterpreted conclusions. He had read and reread in the *Apocrypha* that 'Upon the third day Thou didst command that the waters should be gathered in the seventh part of the Earth; six parts hath Thou dried up ...' And he had concluded that only one-seventh of the globe was therefore covered by sea. Columbus decided that, to make up the other six-sevenths, there must be a vast land mass to the west. The Atlantic Ocean could not be that big, after all!

For years, while sailing the shipping lanes around Portugal and Spain and down the coast of Africa to the Canary Islands, he had been planning an Atlantic crossing. The Italian captain first explained his dream in 1484 to King John II of Portugal. He sought the monarch's patronage for a voyage westward to discover a new route to the spice islands of Asia, which he described as being within easy sailing

Above: *Genoa at the end of the 15th century. Columbus was born here, but he accepted patronage from the Spanish royals to make his questing voyage.*

Opposite: *Explorer and adventurer Christopher Columbus believed a short sortie west from Portugal would lead him to the riches of the Orient.*

Right: *Columbus sets sail from Palos. He bids a fond farewell to his sponsors King Ferdinand and Queen Isabella of Spain.*

Below: *The three-masted* **Santa Maria,** *which bore Columbus and his crew across the Atlantic. It was later wrecked.*

distance. The disbelieving king turned him down.

Eight years later, he put his project to Spain's King Ferdinand and Queen Isabella – and it was accepted.

He assembled a humble fleet of three tiny, wooden-hulled ships in the bustling port of Palos, on Spain's southern coast. On Friday 3 August 1492 a gentle breeze carried Columbus and his 86 fellow seamen out of the harbour.

Led by his flagship, the 70-foot *Santa Maria*, and followed by her attendant vessels the *Pinta* and *Nina*, the small fleet headed for San Sebastian in the Canaries. Then on 6 September, eager not to miss the prevailing easterly winds, the ships turned westward into the open Atlantic.

MUTINY

The great navigator was at last on his way, heading for the greatest discovery – but also one of the biggest blunders – of any explorer.

The crew were more than a little fearful of what lay ahead. They were voyaging beyond the horizon of the known world. The mighty Atlantic Ocean seemed endless. And so it almost proved. The square-rigged ships at first made good progress in the following wind, but by mid-September, with land still not in sight, his men became worried. They feared they might never see Spain again.

The uneducated crew saw no glory in the mission, and they could not give a fig for its commercial aims – to bypass the Moslem-controlled trading routes to the Indies. All they were worried about was their safety and their comfort; few had bunks to sleep on and the inadequate food was already running low. There was even talk of mutiny.

For one man, however, the thought of sailing into the unknown held no terror. Christopher Columbus had no thought of turning back. Instead, perhaps to allay his crew's fears, perhaps doubting his own estimate of the distance to the Indies, he began to keep a false log. From 19 September, in a meticulous manner, he started underestimating the miles his ships were sailing each day.

The *Santa Maria*, the *Pinta* and the *Nina* were sometimes battered by high seas, at other times becalmed for days. They rode out the perils of the Sargasso Sea, and sailed ever west. Columbus was desperate for his expedition to succeed, but he was also mindful of the rewards that would be heaped on him by a grateful king and queen upon his return.

Hopes that the fleet was nearing land were often raised and dashed. More and more seagulls began to show … then land birds. Sadly, the jubilant crewmen were probably deluding themselves that this meant a continent was just over the horizon. Most of the birds they saw were migratory.

On 11 October, however, the men of the *Santa Maria* spotted a green branch floating in the water. And at 2 o'clock the following morning, Rodrigo de Triana, a seaman on board the *Pinta*, raised the cry: 'Land!'

On 12 October, 37 days after leaving the Canaries, the fleet hove to off an island which Columbus named San Salvador (now believed to be Watlings Island in the Bahamas). Elated, he wrote in his log:

'There we soon saw naked natives … A landscape was revealed to our eyes with lush green trees, many streams and fruits of various types.' The next day he wrote: 'I saw that some of the men had pierced their noses and had put a piece of gold through it … By signs, I could understand that we had to go to the south to meet a king who had great vessels of gold.'

MONUMENTAL ERROR

On October 17 he noted: 'On all these days I have been in India it has rained more or less …'

Columbus was referring to the new lands as 'India'. He still thought he had made his landfall on the eastern coast of Asia. And in the light of this monumental

THE ROUGH CREW WHISPERED WORDS OF MUTINY – THEY FEARED THEY'D NEVER SEE THEIR HOMELAND AGAIN.

error, he began his exploration of the New World – firmly believing that the West was the East.

Christopher Columbus sailed among the Caribbean islands until he reached the north coast of Cuba, thence on to Hispaniola (now Haiti and the Dominican Republic). Still believing that the Asian mainland was somewhere over the horizon, he wrote in his log on 28 October: 'I dare to suppose that the mighty ships of the Grand Khan come here and that from here to the mainland is a journey of only ten days.'

The fleet never attempted to reach the unseen 'Asian' mainland. Instead, after eight months at sea, they returned in

Above: *Columbus stopped long enough to raise the Spanish flag on Hispaniola before rushing back to Spain with news of his discovery.*

triumph to Spain, where Columbus was made 'Admiral of the ocean sea and governor of the islands newly discovered in the Indies'.

It was only later, after Spanish and Portuguese voyagers had explored and mapped the Americas, that Christopher Columbus received the posthumous accolade of discovering a new continent. But did this obsessive Italian émigré, hired by a foreign paymaster, really discover the New World?

UNCANNY RESEMBLANCE

Researchers suggest that it is possible that many other races, equipped with vessels far more primitive than his, could have reached it before him. People have been settled in America for 12,000 years – a fact ascertained using carbon dating, a process that accurately pinpoints the date of an artefact or other object to within 100 years.

The first settlers in America were probably descendants of Mongoloid tribesmen who reached the continent by crossing the land bridge across the Bering Strait from Siberia to Alaska. This much we know of the indigenous people, the first Americans. But who were the first people from other continents to reach America?

Some theoreticians claim that the Chinese, who were masters of technical and cultural affairs long before the Europeans, were the first outsiders to land in America. They point to the discovery of sculptures amongst the remains of ancient Central American nations and their uncanny resemblance to idols used in the Buddhist religion as proof that the Chinese arrived there in about 2000 BC. Another people who may have set foot in America before the time of Christ are the Phoenicians. Herodotus, the Ancient Greek historian, mentions the Phoenicians and wrote in 600 BC that sailors of Tyre and Sidon were hired by Pharaoh Necho of Egypt to sail around Africa. They accomplished this astonishing feat, and went on to sail the Atlantic in triremes – galleys with triple decks of oarsmen. It is thought that they reached the Azores, the site of the discovery in the 18th century of a hoard of gold Carthaginian coins.

However, the greatest backing for the claims arises from the discovery of an inscribed stone in a Brazilian coffee plantation in 1872. The translation reads: 'We are sons of Canaan from Sidon, the city of the king. Commerce has cast us on this distant shore, a land of mountains … We voyaged with ten ships. We were at sea together for two years … So we have come here, 12 men and three women on a new shore which I, the admiral, control. But auspiciously may the exalted gods and goddesses favour us.'

Is that proof that Phoenicians discovered the Americas long before the birth of Christ, and of course many centuries before Christopher Columbus? The argument rages to this day – against claims from many other lands and peoples.

CRYSTAL TOWERS

A 6th-century Latin manuscript which has survived contains evidence that the Irish may have been the first Europeans to cross the Atlantic. The *Navigatio Sancti Brendani* tells how St Brendan set sail in AD 540 with a crew of 14 monks. His mission was to 'find the land promised to the saints'. The *Navigatio* says that Brendan was an experienced sailor from Kerry in the west of Ireland and that his primitive boat was a 35-foot ketch, covered with the hides of oxen and greased with butter to keep it waterproof.

The document tells its story in colourful language that some sceptics believe makes it merely a fairy-tale. But, studied closely, it makes sense to many. The vessel took a northerly course, eventually coming across 'a floating tower of crystal' – probably an iceberg, thousands of which litter the northern approaches to America. They went through an area of dense mist – possibly the famous fog-shrouded Newfoundland Banks, where the warm Gulf Stream mixes with the violent Arctic currents. The manuscript does get fanciful, for Brendan claims they were guided by whales and angels disguised as birds before they reached land. The men landed on a tropical island surrounded by clear waters and inhabited by pygmies. This, say those who believe this theory, could have been one of the islands in the Bahamas group. Later he went on to find another land, which may have been Florida.

There is little hard evidence to confirm

HAD THE IRISH SAINT REALLY SAILED TO AMERICA FROM THE EMERALD ISLE IN A PRIMITIVE KETCH COVERED WITH THE HIDES OF OXEN AND GREASED WITH BUTTER TO KEEP IT WATERPROOF?

the claims of this ancient text, and it could be regarded as just fancy, were it not for the fact that the great Norse sailors testify in their sagas that the Irish were indeed the first to reach America. The Viking voyages, made in their famous longboats with imposing prows and shallow sides, are now established as historical fact. The Vikings made their journeys in short legs from Scandinavia, via Iceland and Greenland, establishing settlements en route. They were well supplied, developing a method of preserving their meats by trailing them in the salted water, and drinking water from cowhide pouches.

In the saga recounting the deeds of the great navigator Leif Ericsson, it is recorded that he reached the New World in AD 1000. He called it Vinland, describing it as a land of beauty and contrasting climates. The sagas, not written by him but based on his records, are believed to refer to the area now known as New England.

The discovery some years ago of eight houses, cooking pots, kitchen implements, boats and boatsheds at a site on the northern tip of Newfoundland offers, says Norwegian historian Dr Helge Ingstad, 'the first incontrovertible evidence that Europeans set foot in America centuries before Columbus's voyage of 1492'.

Another find, relating to the Norse adventurers is also the subject of controversy. In 1898 a farmer clearing land at Kensington, Minnesota, came across a stone covered in the characters of a strange language. The Kensington Rune, as it later became known, was said to tell the story of a 30-strong party of Norwegians and Goths who went west from Vinland in 1362, ending with a massacre in which ten of the party were killed. Again, experts are divided as to whether it is the genuine article or a clever fake. But those who believe in its authenticity say that its language is too complex for it to be a crude forgery.

Other finds may offer positive proof of the Vikings' first foothold on the continent. One such is the Newport Tower, in the centre of Newport, Rhode Island. The circular structure is supported on eight columns and could be old enough to have

Above: *Columbus returned to Spain, where he told Queen Isabella he had found a new route to Asia. He was rewarded with the governorship of the newly discovered province.*

been constructed by the Vikings. But some say that the building is merely the remains of a church built by much later, Christian settlers.

SACRIFICIAL TABLE

Among this mass of Irish, Viking and Phoenician contenders for the discovery of America is one more – another Celtic expedition. A desolate place called Mystery Hill in North Salem, north of Boston, consists of a collection of ruins of a kind usually associated with the great megalithic sites of Europe. There are the remains of 22 huts, passageways and cooking pits, and an eerie sacrificial table with a speaking tube through which voices can be projected – presumably for use during macabre ceremonies.

The huge blocks of granite comprising the passageways are held in place by their own weight, and many thousands of artefacts from different periods have been

Right: *The family man. Columbus was father to two sons, Diego and Ferdinand.*

Below: *A map of the four great voyages charted by Christopher Columbus, from a book published in 1889.*

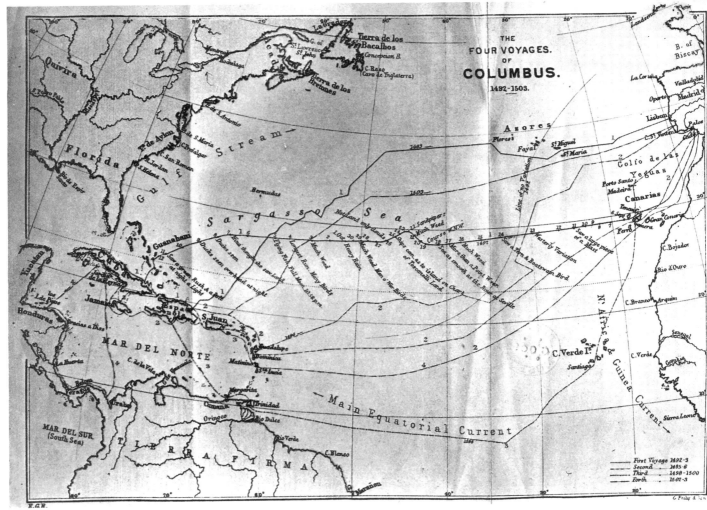

found there. Stones bearing chiselled inscriptions in the ancient Celtic form of rune writing called Ogham have been found too. Is this evidence of yet another race laying claim to America? Or is it perhaps not the work of the Celts, but of Ancient Greeks – perhaps even the great hero of Homer's legendary tale, Odysseus, arriving there on his voyage to the far frontiers of the world? The theories are endless.

What is now certain, however, is that it was not Christopher Columbus who first set foot in the Americas. For centuries, the crediting of the Italian navigator as the founder of the New World has been an astonishing mistake.

Even Columbus himself slowly began to realize that his earliest theories about the land to which he had sailed might be challenged by the evidence of history. In the ten years following his first crossing of the Atlantic, he made three further epic voyages, and only towards the end of his explorations did he begin to doubt whether he had in fact found the eastern coast of Asia.

On his third voyage in 1498 he began to wonder whether he had found a new continent. He had taken a more southerly course across the Atlantic and had made landfall on the island of Trinidad. While exploring in the nearby Gulf of Paria, he came to the place where the mighty Orinoco River of South America flows into the sea. In his log of 14 August 1498, he wrote: 'I believe that this is a very large continent which until now has remained unknown.'

AN IGNOMINIOUS END

In 1502 Columbus set out on his fourth voyage. For nine months, in gruelling weather, he explored the coasts of Honduras, Costa Rica and Panama. Then, in May 1503, he struck north in a desperate bid to reach the new Spanish settlement of Santo Domingo, on the island of Hispaniola. He failed. With his storm-battered ships – worm-eaten, leaking and altogether unseaworthy – he spent 12 months as a castaway on Jamaica before being rescued with his crew and taken back to Spain.

It was an ignominious end to the last

great voyage of the great navigator. He returned home still believing that the islands he had discovered on his first two voyages were off the eastern coast of Asia. He still believed that a passage through to Asia must exist between these islands and the great new land to the south.

Twice he had stumbled across the New World without really knowing it. He died on 20 May 1506, never to know that the land he had discovered was in fact the vast continent of America.

The result of his error was that the land that Christopher Columbus had risked his life four times to reach was named after one of his rivals. Fellow Italian adventurer Amerigo Vespucci explored much of Brazil's coastline – and it was the accounts of his discoveries that eventually won him the honour of having the great new continent named after him.

It is Christopher Columbus, though, who will probably continue to be credited as the man who discovered the New World. He may have made a giant error, but his discovery is part of the history of mankind and paved the way to the modern world. The tragedy for Columbus himself is that he died without ever knowing how stupendous his achievement was.

Above: *Columbus still gets all the credit for discovering the New World, even though there's evidence that ancient peoples made the journey there centuries before he set sail.*

TRAGICALLY HE DIED WITHOUT EVER KNOWING HE'D DISCOVERED ONE OF THE EARTH'S GREAT CONTINENTS.

DAILY SKETCH, MONDAY, OCTOBER 6, 1930.

SURVIVORS' VIVID STORIES OF AIRSHIP DISASTER

DAILY SKETCH

INCORPORATING THE DAILY GRAPHIC

ONE PENNY.

R101 MEMORIAL NUMBER

WONDERFUL AIR PICTURE

MONDAY, OCTOBER 6, 1930.

No. 6,699. (Registered as a newspaper.)

THE LAST OF THE GIANT R101:

...aster in which R101 crashed in flames near Beauvais, Northern France, within eight hours of ...killed, there being only eight survivors. Her commander, Flight-Lieut. H. C. ...another of the victims, initiated the construction of R101 and ...their air vessels.

THE R101
A flight to hell

Lord Thomson of Cardington thought that the world's mightiest airship would carry him to personal glory – blind ambition prevented him from seeing that the R101 would be his ticket to a blazing hell.

The R101 airship was a disaster long in the making. It was designed and built to satisfy the power and prestige of politicians. And it was flown in the face of all advice and protests in order to satisfy the whim of one man. The R101, this mightiest of British inflatables in the age of airships, was used to boost the already over-inflated ego of Lord Thomson of Cardington, the secretary of state for air. His arrogance cost the lives of all but six of its 54 passengers and crew in an inferno on a French hillside in 1930.

The most unnecessary disaster in the history of flying began seven years earlier, however, when in 1923 the Conservative government was persuaded by the Vickers aircraft and engineering firm that giant airships could be used for passenger services linking all major parts of the Empire. The government would commission them and Vickers, the most experienced builders of airships in Britain, would, of course, be paid to build them.

Vickers, greedy for the contract, were horrified when the Conservatives fell before a decision could be made, and in 1924 the first Labour parliament came to power on promises of nationalization and state control. Socialism was the order of the day and success for the fiercely capitalist firm of Vickers was not to its liking.

ASTONISHING DECISION

The new prime minister Ramsay MacDonald and his advisors then made the most astonishing decision. They decided to commission not one, but two airships to exactly the same specification: the R100, a capitalist airship, and the R101, a socialist airship. The R100 was to be built by Vickers and the R101 by the Air Ministry. By some extraordinary set of rules, the government would then decide which of the two would win its accolades and its orders.

No one was more astonished by this than Nevil Shute Norway – now better known as novelist Nevil Shute. At the time, he was Vickers' chief calculator, and he wrote: 'The controversy between capitalism and the state enterprise had been argued, tested and fought in many ways but the airship venture in Britain was the most curious of them all.'

Above: *Lord Thomson, the man who made the success of the R101 a life's ambition.*

Opposite: *Cover of the* Daily Sketch, *which graphically illustrated the scale of the disaster.*

Below: *The R101 was visually stunning but it was plagued by design faults. It should never have left the ground.*

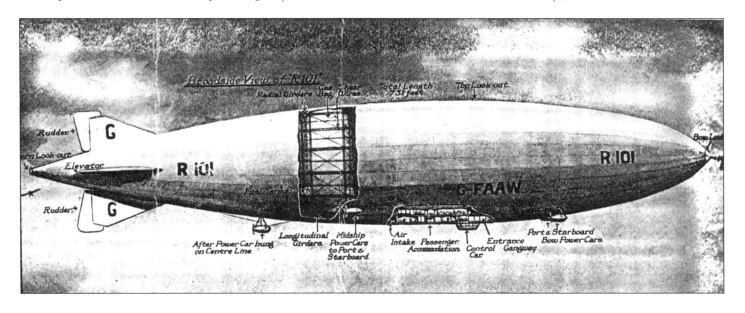

THE DESIGN WAS BEAUTIFUL – AND LETHAL.

Lord Thomson, Labour's air minister, was responsible for the R101. So fanatical about the project was he that he adopted the name of the nationalized aircraft factory as part of his title. It was therefore as Lord Thomson of Cardington that he oversaw the building of the airship at Cardington, near Bedford. The first problem facing the design team was the ministry's decision that petrol engines would be unsafe for their airship. The Cardington team argued fiercely against deisel engines but were overruled. As a consequence, 8-cylinder diesel units were ordered – engines originally designed for railway locomotives. They weighed twice as much as the R100's petrol-power units, were far less efficient and vibrated alarmingly.

Such was the weight of the engines and other equipment built into the R101 that when the airship was first inflated and tested it was discovered that its lifting power was about half what it should have been. The team immediately began taking out of the craft all the gadgetry which they had confidently built into it. The effect was disastrous …

The gas valves were so sensitive that they leaked perpetually. The propellers broke when put into reverse, and a heavy backward-facing engine had to be fitted in order that the airship could manoeuvre when docking. The hydrogen bags which would keep it aloft rolled around inside the craft. The airship was unbalanced. It bucked up and down dangerously as soon as it was tethered at its mooring mast. The craft's outer casing split time and time again and ended up being covered with patches, and the fins, though beautifully streamlined, tended to stall.

Of course, many such problems were also encountered by the Vickers R100 team, led by designer Barnes Wallis, who was to become famous in World War 2 for his dam-busting bouncing bomb. But they were overcome – despite some less than salubrious conditions.

The R100 was being built in a leaky World War 1 airship hangar at Howden, Yorkshire. Writing much later about how untrained local labour was being used for much of the manual work, Nevil Shute complained: 'The local women were filthy in appearance and habits, and incredibly foul-mouthed. Promiscuous intercourse was going on merrily in every dark corner.'

Shute never gave an opinion as to whether this was the reason that the R101 was finished first! But, by hook or by crook, it was and a VIP crowd was invited to Cardington to watch it being floated out of its hangar.

DISASTER AVERTED

A few weeks later, on 28 June 1930, the largest airship in the world – 200 yards long and filled with 5 million cubic feet of hydrogen – was flown to Hendon to take part in an air display … and immediately

Below: *The Royal Airship Works, Cardington, where the ill-fated R101 was constructed.*

Left: *R100 flying over Farnborough. It took longer to build than its government-sponsored rival, but it flew beautifully.*

appeared to embark on a sequence of aerial stunts. It twisted and turned, then suddenly dipped its nose and dived spectacularly before pulling up sharply. The 100,000-strong crowd applauded, but they were even more impressed when moments later the aircraft, already too low for comfort, repeated the manoeuvre and pulled out of its dive just 500 feet above the ground.

The entire show had, of course, been entirely unplanned. The crowds were unaware that the craft's sweating coxswain had been struggling at the controls to avert disaster. Neither were they told that when the R101 was examined afterwards more than 60 holes were found in the hydrogen bags. The highly inflammable gas was pouring out everywhere.

The public was blissfully innocent of these problems. The Air Ministry technicians were frantic in their attempts to solve them. They had already cut their airship in two, inserted an extra gas tank in the middle, put the craft together again and once more hauled it to its mooring tower. Surely the extra lift would solve their problems. But within minutes, the whole skin of the airship began rippling in the wind, and a 90-foot gash opened up along its side. The next step was to begin disposing of every piece of non-essential equipment. Out went the expensive power steering and many of its more luxurious touches.

The R101's outer cover was a constant source of embarrassment. It rotted so quickly that a story went around that the culprits were construction workers who, too lazy to return to ground level, had habitually urinated from the topmost part of the airship. The chemical reaction of urine with the solution of dope on the outer skin was said to have been detrimental. It is known that as the airship emerged from its hangar one day in June 1930, a rip 50 yards long appeared in its side. It was repaired

but exactly the same thing occurred the following day.

At this time one courageous Air Ministry inspector reported: 'Until this matter is seriously taken in hand and remedied I cannot recommend the extension of the present permit-to-fly or the issue of any further permit or certificate.' His report was never published and was quietly pigeon-holed by the ministry mandarins.

Production of the rival R100 was meanwhile continuing apace. The Vickers airship lacked the beautiful lines of its sister craft but had one significant advantage: it could actually fly!

The Vickers team announced that their airship would embark on its flight to Canada in the summer of 1930. The Cardington team suggested a postponement both of the Canada trip and of their trip to India. Vickers, gleeful at their rivals' problems, refused to call off the R100's journey. On 29 July 1930, seven years after

Below: *R101 at its mooring tower. Wind constantly ripped its outer skin and hydrogen poured out of dozens of holes in the gas bags.*

Above: *Sir Sefton Brancker doubted that the R101 could survive a major voyage. He discovered, to his cost, that he was right.*

Below: *The luxurious lounge where passengers relaxed, in ignorance of the problems besetting the ship in flight.*

Vickers first proposed the giant airship project, the R100 set off for Canada. It completed the round-trip successfully and without fuss.

By now, Lord Thomson was beginning to fluster and bluster. He saw his pet project as a battle between capitalism and socialism, a battle that the socialists were losing. It did not help his case that the private-enterprise sister ship had so far cost the taxpayer somewhat less than his R101. The noble lord's airship must not be shown to be second-best. It had to fly – and soon.

Re-covered, lightened and lengthened, the R101 made its trial flight on 1 October 1930. The craft's oil-cooler having broken down, there was no opportunity for any speed trials. Poor-weather tests had not even been embarked on. The airship had not flown at full power. Neither had the R101 been issued with an airworthiness certificate … so the Air Ministry wrote one out for themselves.

HELPLESS!

The very day before the flight, a final conference about the trip was held at the Air Ministry. Lord Thomson piously warned: 'You must not allow my natural impatience or anxiety to influence you in any way.' No one believed his caution was sincere. After all, he had already announced: 'The R101 is as safe as a house – at least to the millionth chance.' And he had issued an official directive to everyone concerned in the project: 'I must insist on the programme for the Indian flight being adhered to, as I have made my plans accordingly.'

Nevil Shute wrote later: 'To us, watching helplessly on the sidelines, the decision to fly the R101 to India that autumn of 1930 appeared to be sheer midsummer madness.' He said of Thomson: 'He was the man primarily responsible for the organization which produced the disaster. Under his control, practically every principle of safety in the air was abandoned.'

But despite dissension among the designers, fears by Air Ministry inspectors and the alarm of the Cardington team itself, the great man would not be swayed. Lord Thomson had other reasons for pressing ahead with his personal flight to India. He wanted to make a magnificent impression when the airship arrived at Karachi. His ambition was to become Viceroy of India and he hoped that the spectacle would help him achieve that aim. And he had to fly straight away because he did not want to miss the Imperial Conference to be held in London in mid-October.

A fellow VIP booked on the flight was not so sanguine. Air Vice-Marshal Sir Sefton Brancker, the monocled director of civil aviation, was extremely sceptical, having been privy to reports on the R101's trials. He had learned that when the airship dived at Hendon it had virtually broken its back. He knew that hydrogen constantly poured from holes caused by the gas bags chafing against each other and the superstructure. But when he voiced his concerns, Thomson told him: 'If you are afraid to go, then don't.' Sadly, Sir Sefton accepted the challenge.

Lift-off from the Royal Airship Works, Cardington, was to be on the evening of 4 October. It was wet and miserable. At 6.30 pm Thomson and his valet stepped aboard. There were four other passengers, plus 48 crew.

STORM CONDITIONS

The leaky airship was so grossly overweight that it had to drop 4 tons of water-ballast to get away. At 8 pm, over London, it received a new weather forecast by radio, predicting a 40 mph headwind over northern France, with low cloud and driving rain. The senior crew member, Major G.H. Scott, grew alarmed. He had successfully captained the R100 to Canada and back, and he knew of the deficiencies of the R101. Yet he had decided to come along 'for the ride'. Knowing that the R101 had never flown in anything but good weather conditions, Scott discussed the radio report with Thomson. What the two men said will never be known, but the airship flew on.

As the rain lashed down on the 777-foot-long airship, the weight of tons of

water slowed it down and made it even more unstable. It rolled and pitched and was flying dangerously low, but inside the vast hull, crewmen went about their business while the passengers slept.

The twin-berth cabins formed the upper deck of a two-floor module sealed off from the roar of the engines and the beating of the weather. On the lower deck was the lounge, 60 feet long and more than 30 feet wide, with wicker settees, chairs and tables, and potted plants disguising the supporting pillars. Outside the lounge ran promenade decks with panoramic observation windows. Also on the lower deck were the ornate dining room, a smoking room and kitchens.

CRASH DIVE

Stairs led down to the control room, slung under the hull, which was the closest point to the ground. As the craft crossed the Channel, the watch noticed the surging seas perilously close beneath them. An officer grabbed the controls and brought the airship back to 1,000 feet.

The winds increased as the R101 crossed the French coast. Observers at Poix airfield estimated her height at only 300 feet. At 2 o'clock in the morning, the R101

Above: *R101 dropping ballast as it struggles to rise. Without the stabilizing weight it rolled and tilted precariously.*

INSIDE THE VAST HULL, CREWMEN WENT ABOUT THEIR BUSINESS WHILE THE PASSENGERS SLEPT.

was over Beauvais in northern France. It had travelled only 200 miles in more than seven hours.

Radio operator Arthur Disley had just turned in after tapping out this message back to Britain: 'After an excellent supper, our distinguished passengers smoked a final cigar and have now gone to rest after the excitement of their leave-taking.' Disley awoke later in his berth and realized something was wrong.

The nose of the R101 had suddenly dipped.

Engineers John Binks and Albert Bell were chatting in one of the gangways. Both fell with a bump. Foreman engineer Henry Leech, alone in the smoking room, slid off the settee. His glass and soda syphon clattered from the table. The R101 righted

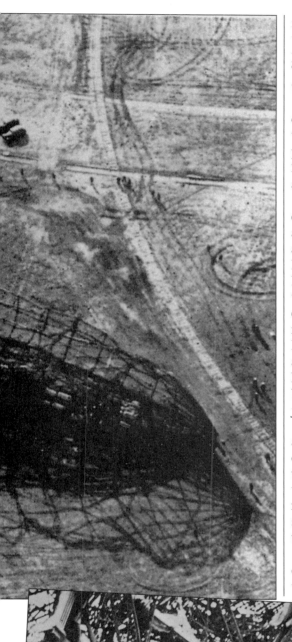

itself and again roared forward against the wind and rain. In the smoking room, Leech picked up the glasses and the soda syphon. They were unbroken. He replaced them on the table and lounged back on the settee.

Down below in Beauvais, several citizens were leaning out of their windows watching the strange airship sail by. It passed over the centre of the town, about 200 yards above the ground. It was rolling and dipping.

In the control car, the watch had just changed. The navigator looked at his altimeter – and was horrified to see that, although it recorded 1,000 feet above sea level, the airship was almost at ground level. The gentle hills around Beauvais were higher than he had thought. The engines were put at half speed and the release of water-ballast was ordered. Rigger Alf Church was walking to the crew area at the end of his term of duty when he heard an officer shout: 'Release emergency ballast.' Church ran back to his post and jettisoned half a ton of water from the nose.

The R101 was once again flying straight and level, but very low. Suddenly the nose dipped for the second time. As the airship's telegraph rang, coxswain Oughton wrestled with the controls. The elevators did not respond. The frail fabric at the nose of the ship had split. The wind was gusting in and the hydrogen was pouring out.

Below the doomed airship, on the edge of a wood, 56-year-old Alfred Roubaille was out poaching, hoping to bag a couple

COVERED IN PERSPIRATION THE COXSWAIN WRESTLED FRANTICALLY WITH THE CONTROLS – BUT THE R101 WAS PLUNGING TO ITS DOOM.

Left: *The charred remains of the death ship R101.*

Below left: *Every shred of fabric on the ship itself was burned, but the RAF flag survived the blaze to flutter forlornly on the wreckage.*

Below: *Air Marshal Salmond joined other dignitaries to survey the wreckage and wonder what had gone so catastrophically wrong.*

of rabbits for his family's Sunday lunch. He plodded across the sodden ground, stopping every now and then to lay his snares. Roubaille heard a roaring of engines above, looked up – and fled to the shelter of the trees. 'The airship started to sink towards the ground,' he later recounted. 'She was moving slowly forward and pointing her nose downwards. Just as the airship was nearing the ground, a strong gust of wind blew her down hard.'

Peering at the looming earth through the window of the control room, the first

Above: *Binks, Bell and Leech in the funeral procession leaving from Beauvais town hall en route to the railway station.*

officer, Lieutenant-Commander Atherstone, realized the airship was doomed. He ordered Chief Coxswain Hunt to race through the hull and alert everyone that the ship was about to crash. 'We're down, lads,' he screamed over and over.

Radio operator Disley heard the warning and swung his legs from his bunk. Leech leapt from the smoking room settee. In the engine-gondolas suspended beneath the

hull, engineers Cook, Bell, Binks and Savory watched horrified as the ground came up to meet them.

Thanks to the crewman in charge of the elevators, who died pulling at the wheel in a bid to make the craft climb, the R101 touched down lightly. One man leaped from a gondola and started running away as fast as his legs would carry him. He did not look back. Only Roubaille the poacher, from his sanctuary beneath the trees, witnessed the entire catastrophe which shook the world.

BLAZING INFERNO

The R101 was blown along the ground, then bounced 60 feet back into the air. Finally, it pancaked into the moist earth of a flat field no more than 100 yards from the poacher. For a moment, the only sound was the gush of escaping gas. Then a blinding flash lit the sky. Two further explosions quickly followed and a white-hot inferno engulfed the world's mightiest airship.

Engineer Henry Leech was still in the

Left: *The ill-fated R101 looked majestic in flight. But a close inspection revealed it wasn't fit to undertake a journey. One man's haste and obsession to win a race led to a series of faults and flaws which went unchecked.*

smoking room when the explosions started rocking the remains of R101. He had just got up from the settee when the blazing metal ceiling crashed down on it. Flattening himself to the floor, he crawled on all fours towards a hole that had opened in the wall and leapt through the flaming envelope of the airship. Once safely outside, he heard the cries of radio operator Arthur Disley still inside the blazing hull. He was clawing at the fabric, even attempting to bite an opening in it with his teeth. Leech ran back into the inferno to help him.

Both Leech and Disley seemed doomed. But then there was a miracle. Suddenly a fiery hole opened up in the hull and the two men flung themselves through it. They landed in wet bushes and raced to safety.

Another lucky crewman was engineer Victor Savory, who was blinded by the flash of flame that roared in through the open door of his gondola. Instead of cowering away from the heat, he bravely leapt for the opening and found himself lying on the soft soil of France.

Crewman Albert Cook also tried to get out of his gondola door but found it blocked by a girder, dripping with blazing cellulose from the hull. He dragged away the girder with his bare hands and hurled himself into the undergrowth below. He was pitifully burned. Recalling the horror later, he said: 'I lay down and gave up – but only for a moment.'

The gondola of engineers John Binks and Albert Bell also became engulfed in flames. They believed they were lost. But then came yet another miracle. A ballast tank above the gondola burst – and the water cascaded onto them, putting out the flames. They were the luckiest to be alive that dreadful night.

Poacher Roubaille could never forget his personal vision of hell: 'I heard people in the wreckage crying for help. I was a hundred yards away and the heat was awful. I ran as hard as I could away from that place.'

Of the 54 people, only six – Savory, Cook, Binks, Bell, Leech and Disley – survived. Lord Thomson of Cardington was among the 48 who died because of his blind ambition.

BEN JOHNSON
The fastest lie on Earth

As Ben Johnson raced to the finishing line and a gold medal on that hot September day he knew he was breaking a world record. The next day he broke a nation's heart.

A hush fell on the Olympic stadium as the world's top athletes lined up for the race of their lives, running for the title of the fastest man on Earth. The crack of a starting pistol shattered the silence. It sent the sprinters towards the finishing line 100 metres away at a breathtaking pelt, their muscles taut and glistening with perspiration, each face a mask of concentration. One man roared off the blocks faster than his rivals. His lightning reaction helped him to finish the race ahead of the field, almost before the echo of the pistol had died.

For Canadian Ben Johnson it was the moment he had dreamed of since childhood when he sped barefoot on a dusty tropical road. Now he was the record-smashing champion of the whole world, no messing. After years of toil and training, here at last was the glory he longed for. The strains of the Canadian national anthem being played in the Olympic stadium in Seoul, South Korea, that steamy Saturday afternoon in September 1988 sounded triumphantly for the athletes of a nation, heralding a future of hope. In reality it was a knell of doom for Johnson.

As he stood on the rostrum to have the coveted gold medallion draped around his neck, Johnson could barely disguise a look of anxiety. He knew he was a cheat.

AN ATHLETIC JUNKIE

Within just a few days, the world shared his shameful secret. A test for drugs used by athletes to enhance their performance proved positive. Johnson's fame turned to infamy and he was stripped of his honours, humiliated in front of his country and the world.

The fair-play fans of field events across the globe might just have forgiven him the acutely public misdemeanour, believing him to be a pawn in the hands of unscrupulous and ambitious trainers and under pressure to be the best.

But the humbling experience of being unmasked as a fraud failed to teach him a lesson for life. Less than five years later he was snared for the same offence and he was banned from competing for life. Now Johnson's only claim to fame is as an athletic junkie who has dragged the reputation of his country and his sport through the mud.

Ben Johnson was born in Falmouth, Jamaica, at the close of 1961, one of five children. At the age of 14 he emigrated with his mum, brothers and sisters to Canada, leaving his dad in Jamaica. While his mum worked as a chambermaid in a Toronto hotel, Johnson discovered he was born to run. His pounding stride easily outstripped the other schoolboys he raced. Before long he was noticed by Charlie Francis, former world-class runner, gymnasium owner and athletics trainer, who realized the teenager possessed enough talent to take him to the top.

His first big league outing on the track, aged 16, was notable only for its singular lack of success. Johnson finished last in

Above: *Once Johnson could walk with his head held high as his country's finest athlete.*

HIS POUNDING STRIDE SOON OUTSTRIPPED THE OTHER SCHOOLBOYS – BEN HAD DISCOVERED THAT HE WAS BORN TO RUN.

Opposite: *Johnson leaves the drug control centre in Hamilton after being caught cheating by taking drugs to enhance his performance – not once, but twice.*

BURNING WITH ENVY AND FRUSTRATION, JOHNSON KNEW HE WOULD DO ANYTHING TO BEAT CARL LEWIS.

Below: *Johnson burned with ambition to beat athletic legend Carl Lewis,* **pictured below.**

Canada's Commonwealth Games 100-metres trial, but he continued his training with grim determination. Just a year later he won the nation's junior title as well as winning citizenship. By now he was running 100 metres in 10.79 seconds.

By 1980 he was fast enough to race in the Olympics, but Canada joined the USA in a boycott of the games brought about by the intervention of the host nation, the USSR, in Afghanistan. It left the way clear for Briton Allan Wells to win gold in the prestige 100-metres event.

But for the first time that year Johnson pitted his speed and strength against Carl Lewis, the American who had made history on the track with his astonishing times. Both competed in the Pan-American Junior Games. Lewis won the 100-metres event; Johnson trailed in sixth place. Lewis's cycle of success spawned a bitter rivalry which bubbled under the surface every time they raced against each other. Lewis was determined to retain his title of undisputed speed king while Johnson was equally driven to snatch the top slot for himself.

Each day Johnson undertook gruelling training sessions in his bid to reach the top of his sport. Each year he edged closer to his goal. In 1981 he was the best runner in his country. The following year he was second to Allan Wells in the Commonwealth Games and by 1983 he made it into the semi-finals of the world championships.

In 1984, Johnson won the bronze medal in the Los Angeles Olympics in the 100-metres event.

The 1984 Games, troubled though they were by the boycott of Iron Curtain countries, had belonged to Carl Lewis, who scored gold in the 100 metres, 200 metres, relay and long jump. Lewis was heaped with accolades, having mimicked the success of the legendary Jesse Owens at the Berlin Olympics, where the affable star was repeatedly snubbed by Hitler because he was black.

Johnson burned with frustration at running once again in the shadow of the great man. He felt sure he could beat Lewis and yearned to prove himself right.

He didn't have long to wait. He claimed victory for the first time against Carl Lewis in the athletics World Cup. Already the bogey of drugs was looming large over the sport. Johnson brushed aside any doubts about his own stance on drug taking: 'I want to be the best on my own natural ability and no drugs will pass into my body.'

ROGUE COMPETITORS

It seemed the tough physical regime he was following had paid off: Johnson was no longer having to settle for second place. He won the Commonwealth and the World Championship titles in consecutive years before the fateful race at the Seoul Olympics. In the World Championships held in Rome in 1987 he not only beat Lewis but achieved a world record of 9.83 seconds. It was the year he won all his 21 races. Again, Johnson's name was linked with drug taking. His camp firmly denied

the suggestion. Coach Charlie Francis said: 'Ben's never taken drugs and never will. Some people do not know how to lose and all they can do is make excuses.' Francis insisted Johnson's astonishing strength came from four hours spent training each day, including 90 minutes devoted to throwing weights.

Olympic officials were increasingly aware of the menace posed by drug takers. The first track competitor to be disqualified after winning a medal was Finnish 10,000-metres runner Martti Vainio in 1984. There was no indication that the problem had been eradicated: if anything, gossip and speculation pointed to widespread use of steroid drugs to increase strength and endurance and cut down recovery time. To sidestep detection, junkie competitors stopped taking the drugs a month before competition. Officials were even thought to be in cahoots with the rogue competitors taking drugs. There was known to be huge profits in it for those who sold the banned substances. Their trade was two-fold: the drug itself, and then an agent which would mask all traces of the illegal dope.

With the prospect of athletes across the board winning only with the aid of chemicals rather than by their efforts alone, the International Olympic Committee was concerned and made testing more rigorous than ever before, banning masking agents and diuretics which can inhibit the processes used to trace drugs. All medal winners and other competitors chosen at random have to give urine samples after their event. The sample is divided into two and stored in sealed containers. One bottle is analysed and if any indications of drugs misuse are found, the second sample is tested with the athlete and a medical representative present.

Before the Johnson scandal erupted, two Bulgarian weightlifters were stripped of their honours and sent home. In addition five other positive tests were taken.

MYSTIFIED

But without doubt the findings in the tests on Johnson were the most sensational. Commentators were still revelling in the excitement and thrill of the race when rumours emerged about Johnson's test result.

A substance called stanozolol was discovered in his urine. It is an anabolic steroid which is like the male hormone testosterone and boosts muscle size, strength and power.

There was outrage among his crew. While Johnson fled Seoul and the glare of publicity, his business manager Larry Heiderbrecht said: 'Ben is obviously sick at the news and will appeal. He is shattered.'

He went on to say that Johnson was probably the most tested sportsman in the world and did not take drugs anyway. There was talk of a blunder in the laboratories, a hoaxer meddling with the sample and the certainty of an appeal.

'It is obvious that something very strange has been happening. Nobody is that stupid to take drugs a few days before a big race. It would appear that the stuff has been in his system for a short period of time.

Above: *Charlie Francis, Johnson's coach, who once said: 'Ben's never taken drugs and never will.'*

Left: *Linford Christie, Britain's record-breaking runner, was horrified to learn his rival Johnson had been a cheat.*

Above: *Johnson bursts through the line in world-record time at Seoul. But his victory was a sham.*

Right: *At the Dubin enquiry in Canada in 1989, which probed the illicit use of drugs in sport, Johnson appeared to be a reformed character.*

THE PROTESTATIONS OF INNOCENCE WERE A SHAM — LIKE THE MAN WHO MADE THEM.

'Ben makes a lot of money from the sport and there is a lot of financial incentive for someone to do something. His training bag could have been left unattended and somebody could have interfered with it. The whole of Canada has been on his back but that would not make him take drugs.'

The people of Canada were mystified. Surely the local boy made good was innocent? After all, drugs testing which had taken place in Montreal before the country's athletes flew to Seoul had failed to pick up signs of abuse.

Even fellow athletes were incredulous at the turn of events. Britain's Linford Christie came third in the race, with Carl Lewis in second place. Although now in line for the silver medal instead of the bronze, he was far from pleased.

'It has been a sad day for athletics,' he said. 'I have never had any suspicion about Ben, he must have been tested over and over again.'

But any hopes of an error were dashed, as Johnson must have known they would be. His protestations of innocence were a sham. His silence was only broken by the smashing of a glass bottle as he threw the illicit substance which had lost him the crown he so desired against the wall of his home.

Later, Carl Lewis claimed he had noticed the sure signs of steroid use before the start of that big race. Johnson's build was stockier than usual, his reactions faster and his eyes yellow. Lewis watched in amazement as Johnson produced some almost superhuman extra pace in the final spurt to victory.

THE FASTEST MAN IN THE WORLD?

Johnson was banned from competing for two years by the International Amateur Athletic Federation and stripped of the world record he clinched at the Olympics of covering 100 metres in 9.79 seconds. A row about whether or not he should ever race again ensued. The Canadian government, which had poured its dreams and cash into the promising career of the young runner, announced Johnson would never again wear its colours. But there was a groundswell of opinion which believed Johnson deserved a second chance. He had been a well-loved national hero who evoked pride and the public's sympathy. Many were convinced he was not only a patsy in the cut-throat world of international athletics, but was also capable of being the fastest man on Earth without using drugs. In fact, Johnson got letters of support not only from Canada but from across the world, along with token gold medals from those fans who felt he deserved the prestige award. His actions as an anti-drugs campaigner in schools and youth clubs around the country also won hearts and minds.

Less than a year later, Johnson talked publicly about the events which led to his disgrace. Speaking at a £3 million inquiry into drug-taking in sport he declared with his characteristic stammer: 'I know what it is like to cheat. I want kids not to take drugs. I also want to tell their parents and families.

'If I get the chance to run again then I will prove I am the best in the world. I will be back.'

He was asked by counsel Robert Armstrong if he thought he could be the fastest man in the world without taking anabolic steroids. He replied: 'I know I can be.' There was spontaneous applause from the public gallery.

Uncomfortably he admitted the statement of innocence made immediately after Seoul was a pack of lies. He said he didn't tell the truth because: 'I was ashamed for my family, other Canadian athletes and the kids who looked up to me. I did not want to tell what the truth was. I was just in a mess.'

His honesty furthered his support by the public, who believed him to be not weak but manipulated, and he was praised for his courage in coming clean. Olympic committee president Juan Antonio Samaranch pronounced that Johnson should not be dealt with any more severely than other competitors found guilty of drugs offences.

Even arch-rival Carl Lewis spoke out against a lifetime ban. There was talk of a multi-million dollar re-match between the two giants when the two-year-ban was ended.

Above: *Juan Antonio Samaranch, president of the International Olympic Committee, knew steroid abuse in sport was probably more widespread than the watching public had realized.*

Below: *Johnson yearned to be the best again following his ban – but he had disappointing results in his first races.*

Canadian TV producer Sheldon Reisler summed it up for many when he said: 'Hell, the only guy in the world who's clean is Eddie the Eagle Edwards [the British ski-jumper who came last in the Olympics]. The world is just saying "Thank God our guy didn't get caught."'

The prospect of him becoming a rich man in the wake of his immorality was hardly mentioned. No one was worried about the lack of an apology or display of repentance or that Johnson seemed to blame his coach, doctor and anyone else but himself.

The sport reeled from the exposé, then set about healing its wounds. Regulations about testing were tightened to ensure they were accurate and penalties against the cheats were increased.

Johnson started training again with a vengeance. He was no longer subsidized by the state but he had something to prove. Trainer Charlie Francis, whose name was so closely linked with the use of steroids in athletics and who was subsequently banned from national athletics, was off the scene. When the two-year ban expired, Johnson found himself a target for the drugs testers who descended on him five times in as many

months, each time producing a negative result. It seemed he had been redeemed.

His preparation for a comeback in January 1991 was accompanied with self-righteous comments such as: 'Steroids must be abolished. They must be treated by the law like heroin, and banned. I am damned glad that I was caught when I was. I didn't feel at ease with my medal anyway.'

Observers noted that he was sleeker, clear-eyed and far more relaxed than the Ben Johnson who was hooked on drugs. But rarely do sprinters surpass their best when they are in their late 20s or early 30s as Johnson by now was. He struggled to pack more power into his 5-foot-11-inch tall frame. When he returned to competition in the Copps Coliseum in Hamilton, Ontario, something vital was missing: the winning streak. Johnson appeared to have lost the stunning start from the blocks which gave him a devastating advantage over other runners. He came in second in a 50-metres race to America's Daron Council, ironically a former narcotics agent.

There was talk of Johnson spending too much time in bars instead of training on the track. But more worryingly, the message

the result appeared to broadcast was that the only way for Johnson to be the best was to take drugs.

Johnson struggled to regain winning form. It was crucial to a man who disliked coming second but still the raw edge of speed which he had once known – albeit through a chemical reaction – eluded him.

A PHONY

At the Barcelona Olympics in 1992 Johnson steered clear of the steroids scandal which this time shamed three British competitors, including Jason Livingston – nicknamed 'Baby Ben' after the fallen athletics idol. But if he thought he would leave Spain with a repaired image he was wrong. This time it wasn't steroids – it was a temper tantrum which let him down.

As the Games drew to a close Johnson wandered into the athletes' village without the mandatory security clearance. The young Spanish volunteers tried to explain they were only doing their job for the protection of all athletes at the Games. In the row which followed, Johnson was accused of punching one of the teenagers. Afterwards, he was sent home with new disgrace heaped on his muscular shoulders. His performance was as disappointing as his behaviour.

After a year of second-rate results, the winning formula was discovered again. Critics were quick to notice it coincided with the reappearance of Charlie Francis during his training sessions. Francis insisted he was only running into Johnson because his wife, hurdler Angie Coon, was working out at the same place.

Warning bells rang, however, when Johnson pulled out of Canada's national event in February 1993 as a result of injury and was not selected for the world indoor championships in March.

The storm clouds were gathering and finally burst open when a newspaper revealed Johnson had been tested positive for a second time. A urine sample taken after an indoor meeting in Montreal in January showed a high level of testosterone. It measured a ratio of 10.3 to one when six to one is considered a positive test.

Dr Arne Ljunqvist, head of a 5-strong

commission which dealt with the test, said: 'I can see no reason and no grounds on which the results can be contested. This is a clear-cut case of testosterone doping.'

Johnson remained behind the closed doors of his £400,000 detached house on the outskirts of Toronto, refusing to talk to reporters. His spokesman declared: 'Mr Johnson denies taking any prohibited substance or engaging in any improper practice since his return to competition.' But Johnson must have realized any denial from his own lips would have sounded hollow. He knew he was to be banned for life.

Above: *Johnson with Francis, the coach who oversaw his international disgrace.*

HUMILIATED BY HIS LACK OF SUCCESS, JOHNSON'S MONSTROUS DESIRE TO WIN SMOTHERED HIS BETTER JUDGEMENT.

Over page: Johnson remains haunted by his infamy.

Once again, he had been proved to be a phony: the faith put in him by the Canadian people was misguided, the forgiveness they showed him misplaced. British athletics coach Frank Dick said: 'This is very sad for the Canadian public who had forgiven Johnson once and are now having it thrown back in their faces. The man must be crazy.'

Canada's sports minister Jean Charest said Johnson had 'perverted the playing fields and hurt the sincerity of all the thousands of athletes who participate fairly'.

The only course left for the man whose glittering career was ended twice in the same shabby way was a silent withdrawal into obscurity, aged only 31. His international notoriety was now enough to shut any door in his face. Plans to blow the lid off the world of athletics where shiny syringes were as vital as clean socks collapsed like a damp squib. It was an undistinguished end to a fiasco.

The affair soured more than just one man's life and dream of being extra special. That vision was left in tatters, like the existence of the man himself. His actions caused wholesale damage to the integrity of a sport from which it may never recover.

Other athletes found themselves struggling to convince onlookers they were not only clean of drugs but worthy of the accolades they had won. Ben Johnson not only exposed the scourge of drugs in sport but illustrated how they were a positive benefit to anyone wishing strongly enough to win. He gave the lie to the old saying 'cheats never prosper'. Honest athletes are pushing for blood testing to eliminate cheats like Johnson, who can sometimes duck detection by using drugs which disguise illegal substances. Trying to make the best of it, Frank Dick remarked: 'Ben Johnson did a great service when he was caught in Seoul. It concentrated everybody on winning this war.'

But even now no one is convinced the sport is squeaky clean. It's been left to red-faced officials to limit the damage as best they can to ensure there is a future for athletics. Johnson, the man who wanted to bring honour to the sport, ended up bringing it to its knees.

MILITARY BLUNDERS

SCHWARZKOPF'S TACTICS WERE BRILLIANTLY SIMPLE: HE HAD LEARNT THE HARD WAY THAT AN ARMY WITHOUT AIR COVER WOULD SOON BE AN ARMY DEFEATED.

Safe in their positions of power, too often military leaders throw away the lives of their solders in their lust for victory. It is not their blood which stains the desert sands bright red and makes the seas and rivers bleed with anguish.

Right above: *Stormin' Norman Schwarzkopf, Commander-in-chief of Operation Desert Storm and a superb military tactician.*

Below: *Saddam in 1980 at the height of Iraq's war with Iran. In this address to his soldiers he assured them Iran would 'surrender or die'.*

Saddam Hussein's attack on Kuwait in 1990 was one gigantic blunder. How did he ever imagine that he could defy the world, especially once it became clear war was looming? Whatever Saddam's tortured reasoning, Iraq's doomed invasion has been quickly consigned to history as one of the most spectacular military failures of the 20th century.

And yet the Gulf War, which cost so few Allied lives, could have turned out so differently. True, the final result would certainly have been victory for the American-led coalition with its dazzling array of hi-tech weaponry. But had Saddam been a true, all-round tactician, Iraq would certainly have given a far better account of herself.

As the commander of Operation Desert Storm, General Norman Schwarzkopf, put it at the end of the war: 'Saddam is neither a strategist, nor is he schooled in the operational arts, nor is he a tactician, nor is he a general, nor is he a soldier. Other than that, he's a great military man.'

Saddam's problem was that he had learnt all his war-lore from the Soviets. He regarded battles as something to be fought on the ground and, ideally, from entrenched defensive positions. 'Let them come to us' could have been his motto. Had he had a more balanced military force, those tactics would undoubtedly have brought about the deaths of many more Allied soldiers. But Saddam Hussein didn't have balance. As it turned out, he didn't really have an air force.

And it was the air war, which began on 17 January 1991, that assured the Allies victory. Time and again during his meet-the-press sessions at Allied Command HQ in Riyadh, Saudi Arabia, Schwarzkopf would stress this. As a front-line Vietnam veteran he knew the effect day after day of bombing had on an enemy's morale and psyche. He had learned one of the great lessons which emerged from World War 2 strategy: an army without air cover would soon be an army defeated.

In his summing up of Allied tactics at the end of the conflict Schwarzkopf admitted that he was worried about the balance of ground forces. At the time US intelligence (wrongly, it turned out) had

predicted a defensive force of well over half a million. The Allies' fighting troops, as opposed to logistic support, was roughly half that. Schwarzkopf knew that in modern warfare an attacking army driving against heavily entrenched positions needed a five-to-one superiority of manpower. He explained how he redressed the balance.

'What we did, of course, was start an extensive air campaign ... one of the purposes was to isolate the Kuwaiti theatre of operations by taking out all the bridges and supply lines that ran between the north and the southern part of Iraq. That was to prevent reinforcement and supply coming into the southern part of Iraq and the Kuwaiti theatre.

'We also conducted a very heavy bombing campaign, and many people questioned why. This is the reason. It was necessary to reduce those [Iraqi] forces down to a strength that made them weaker, particularly along the front-line barrier that we had to go through.'

He went on: 'I think this is probably one of the most important parts of the entire briefing I can talk about. As you know, very early on we took out the Iraqi Air Force. We knew that he had very, very limited reconnaissance means. Therefore,

when we took out his air force, for all intents and purposes we took out his ability to see what we were doing down here in Saudi Arabia.'

AIR BOMBARDMENT

What Schwarzkopf did was move his main ground-attack forces as far west as possible to outflank the Iraqis and meet them where their defences were weakest. The 5-week air bombardment had left Saddam's troops in no real state to fight. The first attack alone, which lasted only three hours, dropped 18,000 tons of explosives on Iraq – twice the amount that razed Dresden and roughly equal to the power of the Hiroshima atomic bomb.

So how did the Iraqi High Command allow the Allies to take control of the skies almost unchallenged by their own warplanes? It wasn't that their aircraft were a poor match. Most experts agreed that Iraq's squadrons of Soviet-built MiG-29 fighters were technically superior – even to America's awesome F-15 Eagles. As for Britain's Tornado interceptors, it would, as one RAF man put it, 'have been like putting up a robin to fight a kestrel'.

Neither was it down to training. Most Iraqi airmen had been taught alongside the

Below: *Tracer fire lights up the night sky during the opening of the Allied air attack on Baghdad. But where was Saddam's air force?*

Above: *Aftermath of an air raid. With total control of the skies Allied bombers rained destruction on Baghdad.*

THE RAF TORNADOS HAD THE HEAVIEST LOSSES – BUT THEY WERE THE PILOTS FORCED TO TAKE THE GREATEST RISKS.

---

very people they were now being asked to shoot out of the sky. They were as competent and intelligent as their adversaries. There was just one important difference – they didn't have the will to fight. Instead of wreaking havoc among the incoming Allied fighters they rarely even engaged them in combat.

Part of the problem was that these airmen were never really trusted by Saddam and he had little interest in either the concept of air battles or the tactical importance of supremacy in the skies. He knew where he stood with ground troops, men who had lived their lives under his leadership, who readily bought the Ba'ath Party line and who had not been tainted with Western ideals. Fliers were a different breed. Their foreign training had given them a fresh outlook on life and they were not the type to obey orders blindly without thought for themselves. Sure enough, when the chance came, they were off.

Ten days into the war the first reports began filtering through of Iraqi planes landing in Iran. The Americans claimed 24 had gone, the Iranians said only seven. Whatever the truth, the trend had been set and more and more were soon fleeing across the border. By 29 January Israel's defence minister Moshe Arens said all 25 of Iraq's Soviet-designed Sukhoi-24 bombers were in Iran. And a few days later

it was claimed more than 150 of Saddam's most modern fixed-wing aircraft were parked up inside the territory of his detested neighbour.

The first wave were clearly defectors. Iran's UN ambassador talked of pilots arriving in his country 'to save their lives and their aircraft' and judging by the way four planes crashed before reaching the border, their fuel tanks empty, it seems Iraqi pilots were prepared to risk a great deal to avoid a scrap with the Allies. Later, Iraqi officials claimed Iran had offered Saddam the use of neutral airfields to protect his air force from total destruction.

The theory has never quite rung true. For a start Saddam is known to have placed airplanes in the centres of towns and villages, knowing the Allies would not risk civilian casualties. Why should he then entrust billions of pounds' worth of hardware to an old enemy he fought for eight long years? And when Iraqi deputy prime minister Sadoun Hammadi was sent to Tehran to make enquiries about the missing air force he was told bluntly that Saddam should have asked permission for his warplanes to enter Iranian air space. As he failed to do this, Iran had a duty to impound them.

Back in Iraq the night skies still echoed to the sound of incoming bombers. RAF Tornados took some of the heaviest losses – seven planes went down during the war – but this was partly connected to their very high-risk end of the operation. Their job was to come in low – at barely 80 feet – and pepper Iraqi airfields with a cocktail of bombs and delayed-action anti-personnel mines. Iraqi gunners may have got three of them; the other four went down because of various technical failures.

On the whole Saddam's anti-aircraft gunners put up a pretty feeble show. They didn't dare turn on their own radar because attacking planes picked up a 'lock-on' instantly and immediately fired off their own HARM missiles which travelled down the incoming radar beam to the AA battery which originated it. As a result many batteries switched off their radar-guidance systems and ended up firing blind into the night sky.

On 30 January, General Schwarzkopf confirmed that he had total control of the skies above Iraq. The operation had taken exactly two weeks and it had gone better than anyone could have dreamed possible. Senior Allied officers made great play of their so-called 'smart' bombs which could be guided onto their target through their own internal sensors. One piece of video tape showed an Iraqi lorry driver motoring across a bridge seconds before a massive bomb smashed it in two. The 'luckiest man in Iraq' was how the briefer described him to Western TV viewers.

If the Allies' public relations policy was going reasonably well, Iraq's was in tatters. Saddam might have hoped to try and lure at least some world opinion onto his side, but if that was his plan he had a funny way of going about it. Exhibiting captured Allied airmen on his national TV caused a wave of revulsion around the globe and merely stiffened the West's resolve to teach him a lesson. In strictly political terms it was a blunder to rival his half-hearted commitment to air defence.

The two British airmen who appeared on Iraqi TV were John Peters and Adrian Nichol, whose Tornado was shot down over the Kuwaiti border on the first day of the war. Peters's face was badly knocked about – he had been beaten by his captors – and he seemed to be contorted in his seat. He was able to answer few questions except to confirm he had been shot down by a missile. Nichol, a burly-looking man with the Union Jack flag clearly outlined on his bottle-green uniform, went a little further.

Questioner: What was your mission?
Nichol: To attack an Iraqi airfield.
Questioner: How were you shot down?
Nichol: I was shot down by an Iraqi system. I do not know what it was.
Questioner: What do you think about the war?
Nichol: I think this war should be stopped so we can go home. I do not agree with this war on Iraq.

Other pilots, among them Americans and Italians, were exhibited in a similar way. It did not go down well with the folks back home. Suddenly a huge weight of pressure was off the Allied political leadership as the pictures caused a massive swing of public opinion against Iraq. Now the voices crying for an end to the war in Britain and America were out on a limb. Saddam had attempted a high-risk gamble, presumably

to boost the morale of his own countrymen, and had ended by digging himself even deeper into the mire.

By early February, Iraq's much-vaunted tank battalions were being picked off in the manner of a duckshoot. Aircraft such as the A10 tankbuster found them easy meat while the Americans' Apache attack helicopters inspired such fear that even the sight of them in the sky caused some Iraqis to desert their posts. One story which found its way back to Allied ground troops, before the assault to liberate Kuwait, came from an Iraqi prisoner-of-war. He revealed how 12 tanks were drawn up together inside Kuwait when one commander spotted an incoming Apache on the horizon. He radioed to all his crews to stay put – intelligence reports showed the helicopter needed to be much closer before it was in range.

Seconds later six of the tanks were simultaneously blown to smithereens in the Apache's first withering salvo. The survivors in the other tanks didn't wait for an explanation from their commander. They fled their posts in time to watch the helicopter finish the job.

THE FINAL CASUALTY?

When the final 'Big Push' arrived – the launching of a ground attack on 24 February – General Schwarzkopf was again

Above: *Flight Lieutenant Adrian Nichol as he appeared on TV under interrogation. It was another blunder by Saddam, in that the British and American viewers saw their 'boys' being humiliated and demanded vengeance.*

IN THE FIRST WITHERING SALVO OF FIRE THE SIX TANKS WERE BLOWN TO SMITHEREENS – THE TERRIFIED SURVIVORS FLED FOR THEIR LIVES.

Above: *Saddam with his 'human shield' of European hostages. He believed sending these TV pictures to the West would help his public relations campaign. Nothing could have been further from the truth.*

able to turn the Iraqis' stubborn military dogma against them. Saddam had assumed from the outset that the assault on Kuwait would come from the sea. He stationed ten Iraqi divisions along the coast and planted thousands of mines along the length of the shore. When his generals reported in early February that the Allied fleet, headed by the vintage battleships *Wisconsin* and *Missouri*, was bombarding Iraqi positions he saw this as evidence that his early assumptions were right.

The dawn of 24 February seemed to confirm it. Egyptian, Saudi and Syrian troops, backed by the US marines, advanced into southern Kuwait while the US 1st Cavalry moved in from the south-west. The Iraqis' 3rd Corps assumed this was the main thrust and moved to intercept. They could not have been wider of the mark.

In fact the attack was coming from the west, spearheaded by heavily armoured American and British divisions. The Iraqis could never have known that such a vast body of men had moved into a totally new attack position within a few weeks. When last their air reconnaissance had checked, virtually the entire Allied camp was concentrated on Kuwait's southern flank.

After that, of course, they lost their air force. They had no eyes.

The ground war was won, comfortably, inside 72 hours. Many of the advancing Allied regiments found their outflanked enemy dug in and facing the wrong way. The Iraqi army, trumpeted weeks earlier by Saddam as the world's fourth biggest, was blown away like leaves before a hurricane.

In the years since the Gulf War many have argued that Schwarzkopf's campaign was a failure in that it failed to knock Saddam from power. Yet that was never the general's brief. His political masters were able to give him only one command and that was to free Kuwait. Any officially backed assassination attempt would have thrown the United Nations into total turmoil.

But if Saddam survived, it was a shaky survival. His two glaring blunders of the war – failing to mount an air defence and failing to guard his western flank properly – had humiliated him in front of his generals. Only the fear he managed to inspire in his High Command helped him avoid a coup.

There was a third blunder. Halfway through the conflict Saddam decided on a half-cocked attempt to drag in the rest of the Arab world. He fired a series of Scud missiles against Israel and succeeded in terrorizing the civilian population. It seemed certain that Israel would lose patience and strike back. Only enormous pressure from the Bush administration in America persuaded her not to.

But the Israelis have long memories. Their secret service, the Mossad, is regarded as the most effective and efficient in the world. There can be little doubt that Saddam Hussein remains high on their list of scores to be settled.

He could yet be the final casualty of the Gulf War.

THE FALL OF SINGAPORE

It was heralded as an island fortress which would never succumb to invading armies, but thanks to blundering British commanders, a tenacious foe and the epidemic of chaos and fear, Singapore fell into the hands of the Japanese with chilling speed.

The embarrassing defeat was a devastating blow to the Allies, who saw yet another prized jewel snatched from under their noses. More than that, there were horrendous casualties among the civilian and military populations. Seventy thousand British and Australian troops were forced to surrender. In February 1942 the city of Singapore was reduced to blazing rubble.

Churchill called it 'the worst disaster and largest capitulation in British history'.

But only afterwards was the extent of the military mismanagement of the campaign to keep Singapore revealed. The Japanese commander, General Tomoyuki Yamashita, declared: 'My attack on Singapore was a bluff. I had 30,000 men and was outnumbered more than three to one. I knew that if I had been made to fight longer for Singapore I would have been beaten. That was why the surrender had to be immediate. I was extremely frightened that the British would discover our numerical weakness and lack of supplies and force me into disastrous street fighting. But they never did. My bluff worked.'

Singapore lies at the south of the Malaysian peninsula and was acquired for the East India Company by Sir Stamford Raffles in 1819 from the Sultan of Johore. Although just 20 miles long and 10 miles wide, it went on to become a busy trading post and naval base for the British in southeast Asia.

It was two months after Pearl Harbor – when the might of the American navy was crippled in dock by a Japanese air onslaught – that the battle for Singapore got under way. A sizeable force of Allied troops had been chased down the Malay Peninsula and into Singapore by the beginning of February. Inexplicably, the island remained poorly defended, despite

> SINGAPORE DID NOT FALL BECAUSE OF JAPANESE MILITARY MIGHT; SINGAPORE FELL BECAUSE OF BRITISH MILITARY INCOMPETENCE.

Left: *Iraqi tanks roll through the streets of Kuwait. They were part of a huge army left defenceless by Saddam's pathetic air cover.*

FEARING THAT THE JAPANESE SOLDIERS WOULD GO ON A VICTORIOUS DRUNKEN RAMPAGE, THE GOVERNOR OF SINGAPORE ORDERED ALL THE ALCOHOL ON THE ISLAND TO BE DESTROYED.

the expansionist, imperial policies of the Japanese so forcefully advertised in Hawaii.

Only in January 1942 did British war leader Winston Churchill learn about the lamentable state of Singapore's defences. Immediately he ordered the island to be fortified to the hilt. 'Not only must the defence of Singapore Island be maintained by every means but the whole island must be fought for until every single unit and every single strongpoint has been separately destroyed. Finally, the city of Singapore must be converted into a citadel and defended to the death. No surrender can be contemplated,' he told war leaders. Wise words, but they came too late to change the destiny of the island.

Yamashita had his sights set on Australia and was keen to steamroller ahead before the morale of his men dipped or they ran short of supplies. He began with a wave of air strikes which devastated the weakening Allied forces on the ground. The British commanders, General Wavell and General Arthur Percival, were at odds through most of the brief campaign to keep the island secure. Wavell thought the attack would come from the north-west. Percival believed the invasion would be in the north-east and posted his best troops there. On 8 February Wavell was proved to have been the better tactician.

When the Japanese landed, the Australian defenders of the area could have surprised them with a blaze of spotlights and pinned them to the beach. But the order to switch on the lights never arrived after communication links were broken. As the enemy marched in, the Australians fell back and a counter-attack never came.

It was the first of many landings. Determined Japanese soldiers took to small boats and dinghies to cross the Johore Strait which divided their island goal from the conquered mainland. Some even swam the short, shallow distance. The defenders of Singapore were in disarray, hit by falling spirits, an active fifth column of Japanese residents on Singapore and the hopeless lines of communication.

It was the last, vital factor that spelled the inevitability of defeat for the Allies. For when the Australians were at last experiencing success in fending off the waves of Japanese soldiers on one shoreline, they were ordered to pull back. It allowed the enemy to flood in unopposed. Subsequent attempts at a counter-offensive by the Allies were bound to fail. By now the troops were utterly downhearted and beleaguered as much by the inadequacy of their own commanders as by the formidable warriors from the land of the rising sun.

In Singapore city there was mayhem. Streams of refugees had flooded in and sought shelter and food where they could. Buildings were still blazing from previous air attacks, dead bodies lay uncollected in the streets. Water supplies were falling fast and the risk of serious disease loomed. There was a frenzied scrabble to board boats leaving the besieged island. The governor of Singapore ordered all liquor to be destroyed so that Japanese soldiers could not go on a victorious drunken rampage when they arrived. Oil storage tanks were set on fire by the British themselves, anxious this valuable commodity should not fall into the hands of the advancing enemy. The intense furnace produced black rain which fell over the crumbling city.

By 15 February, seven short days after the island's defences were first breached, Singapore fell. A package was air-dropped to Percival's headquarters, falling to the ground in a flutter of red and white ribbon. Inside was a message from Yamashita advising him to surrender. It ended with the sinister sentence: 'If you continue resistance, it will be difficult to bear with patience from a humanitarian point of view.'

Percival felt he had no choice. He met the slight victor at the island's Ford assembly plant to sign away the vital outpost. The dream was shattered. Britain could no longer boast that she would successfully defend her colonies, no matter where they were in the world. The brutality of the Japanese invaders against captured British and Australian forces is well recorded, and bitterness about the slavery, torture and terrible conditions the men had to endure is still evident even today. Singapore stayed in the hands of the Japanese until their leader Emperor Hirohito was himself forced to surrender, in August 1945.

THE MASSACRE OF A GENERATION

World War 1 was littered with blunders, each costing countless thousands of lives. The conflict started with an assassination which led to miffed national leaders on both sides embarking on a course of protectionism and revenge. The commanders who held sway were old men with a theoretical rather than practical knowledge of warfare: it was the era when the military man judged most successful was the one who didn't lose his nerve in the face of mounting casualties. Any officer foolish enough to advocate withdrawal to save lives would risk the wrath of his political paymasters and would surely lose his job. So it came about that dogged men who prolonged the slaughter by staying put – even if that meant a mounting death toll and no advance – won the day.

In fact, there was comparatively little troop movement in World War 1. Across Europe, the sides met in head-on confrontation, found themselves equally matched and dug in defensively for a long, drawn-out war of attrition. Trench warfare was both demoralizing and degrading for fighting soldiers, who had to endure the most appalling conditions. The most they died for was a few feet of land.

Offensives in which men were sent over the top into no man's land were largely unsuccessful but were repeated time and again by the military leaders. Both British and German soldiers had the occasional triumph in breaking through the lines of defence, but once it was achieved there was no further plan in existence to capitalize on the gain. As men and officers hesitated, the enemy rallied and the gap was closed once more in their faces. Stalemate resumed. British officers were so incompetent that on at least one occasion they released gas when there was no wind and gassed their own men.

The terrible bloodshed of this military mismanagement left Flanders awash with the dead and wounded. Names like the Somme, Verdun, Passchendaele and Ypres will always be linked with aimless slaughter which claimed the flower of a generation. And for four years the killing went on, without a change in tactics to stem the flow of massacres. Nowhere was the pointless sacrifice of young men at the hands of their blundering leaders more starkly apparent than during the Gallipoli campaign of 1915.

Turkey came into the war specifically to take a swipe at its old imperial enemies, Great Britain and Russia. It lost about

Above: *Churchill strides to his office at the outbreak of World War 1. He was then First Lord of the Admiralty.*

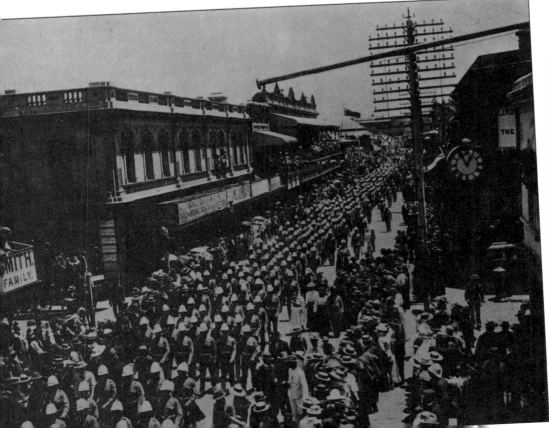

Left: *Australian troops march down the High Street at Freemantle to prepare for embarkation.*

70,000 out of a 100,000-strong army when it attacked Russian troops in the Caucasus, mainly through bitter weather conditions. Regardless of their victory, the Russians appealed to London for a diversion to relieve the pressure on its forces from the armies of the sprawling Ottoman Empire.

GALLIPOLI – A SEA OF BLOOD

The plan to strike at Turkey through the Dardanelle Straits – with an eventual goal of capital Constantinople – was inspired. The waterway which linked the Mediterranean with the Black Sea was clearly vital strategically. Gallipoli was the strand of land on one side of it. With comparative ease, the campaign should have opened up a second front for the German forces, a back door by which to tear into Kaiser Wilhelm II's troops. It was championed by the First Lord of the Admiralty, Winston Churchill.

There was a hopeful start for the British navy, who sailed into the Dardanelles in February 1915, blasted away at the outer fortifications and encountered little resistance. British marines even landed on the Gallipoli peninsula without difficulty.

But the British failed to capitalize on the element of surprise and withdrew the warships into the Aegean, having all but announced their intentions to the Turks. It gave the enemy six valuable weeks to re-arm and reinforce its scanty troops there. There was even the opportunity to mine the straits which had hitherto been a clear passage.

In March the attacking British ships sailed once again on Turkey, this time penetrating the narrow straits. Disastrously, two British battleships and one French were sunk by mines. Churchill was still determined to forge ahead with the operation despite the setback.

In the early hours of 25 April 1915 the largest amphibious force the world had ever known headed for the Gallipoli beaches. In charge was the gentlemanly Sir Ian Hamilton, without a proper map and with no information about the state of Turkish defences more recent than 1906.

Below: *Allied troops at Anzac Cove. A bloodbath lay ahead.*

tenths of the 2,000-strong invading force. The pilot of a spotter plane which flew over the beach that morning described the sea as 'a horrible sight, absolutely red with blood'.

Close by, a further 2,000 men landed on another beach without a shot being fired. They climbed the cliffs and explored the scrubland at the top as they awaited orders. Their officers asked permission to advance. They were poised to mount an attack on the forces pinning down their comrades just a short distance away. Permission was refused. They spent the day in limbo exposed in the open until Turkish troops pounced on them. The surprise engagement forced the British men back down the cliffs and to the water's edge where, in the absence of any direction from their commanders, they evacuated.

*Left: **General Sir Ian Hamilton. He led the largest amphibious force the world had ever seen onto the beaches of Gallipoli, yet he had no intelligence regarding the Turkish defences that was less than nine years old – not even a proper map.***

His position throughout the bloody and lengthy battles to come was to cruise the sea nearby in a large, safe ship. None of his men was warned about the terrain he would be facing, or had landed on a hostile coast like this before.

There were to be various landing points and a further diversionary skirmish staged by the French at Kum Kale on the other side of the Dardanelles. This, it transpired, was to be the single success of the expedition. The 1,500 Australians and New Zealanders who before dawn tumbled out of small boats onto the beach in the first assault were no more than barely trained reservists. In the gloom they realized for the first time there were sheer cliffs ahead of them instead of sloping beaches. Even as they were landing, a hail of bullets rained down, killing many men before they even made it to the beach. Then the guts of the survivors won the day. In the face of an onslaught from enemy fire and then a wave of Turkish fighters who appeared on the beach, the colonial troops fixed bayonets and forced the Turks back up the hill from which they had come. The site of the landing was known thereafter as Anzac Cove, by way of tribute to their courage.

British troops then emerged at Cape Helles from the bowels of a workaday collier boat which appeared to Turkish eyes to run aground by accident, but when they saw the soldiers swarming out of the disabled craft, the Turkish fighters were quick to respond and wiped out about nine-

Columns of troops did successfully breach the Turkish defences but lacked direction to make their gains effective. By midday on 26 April about 30,000 men had landed on the Gallipoli peninsula with little or no gain. General Sir William Birdwood, in charge of the Anzacs now besieged in hopeless conditions on the narrow shale beach beneath the Turkish-controlled heights, implored Hamilton to pull them out. But spurred on by the success of an

*Above: **Troops landing at Gallipoli. They faced impossible terrain ahead and the Anzac commander begged Hamilton to pull the men out.***

Above: *British troops in camp on the Gallipoli peninsula.*

Australian submarine in the Dardanelle Straits, Hamilton refused the plea with the advice: 'there is nothing for it but to dig yourselves right in and stick it out'.

Thus the now familiar trench warfare came to the Mediterranean with conditions every bit as foul as those in France and Belgium. There were few medical supplies and ammunition stocks were low. At Anzac Cove, the men were rationed to two bullets a day. Reinforcements were sent to the British and Australasian forces, just as they were to the Turkish side – now under the leadership of Mustapha Kemal, a future leader of the country.

On 18 May there took place the bloodiest conflict of the campaign with the Anzac Cove men being subjected to the most ferocious assault they had experienced. The Turks tried to overwhelm the Anzac trenches – to be met with volleys of bullets. At the end of the attack, 10,000 Turks were dead or dying in no man's land. It was more than the hardened fighters could bear. On 20 May they raised a Red Cross flag above the front line. It was shot into tatters. But moments later a young

Right: *These men of the 2nd Royal Naval Brigade were among the few troops who got to practice their assault landings. Here they are shown emerging from a trench in a mock attack on the island of Imbros.*

Turkish soldier emerged from the trenches, stumbled over to the Anzacs and, in faltering French, apologized for the killings. After he retreated, Red Crescent flags (the Eastern equivalent of the Red Cross) were raised by the Turks. It paved the way for an informal meeting of commanders who were later able to negotiate a cease-fire. On 24 May each side began the grim task of burying its dead in mass graves.

The truce was to end at 4.30 pm. Half an hour beforehand, the opposing soldiers met and exchanged gifts of cigarettes, fruit and mementoes. After some small talk, they shook hands, parted and returned to their respective trenches. Moments later the shooting started once more.

SCOT-FREE

Frustrated at the stalemate, politicians in London demanded another assault on Gallipoli. This time it was to come at Suvla Bay. Around 20,000 men overran the beach, making short work of the 1,000 Turks there to defend it. In charge, General Stopford, Lieutenant Governor of the Tower, was delighted. He congratulated his men before settling down for his afternoon

nap. The soldiers were allowed to swim and frolic in the sea. By the time Stopford was ready to advance the following day, the Turks had reassembled a strong army which stood in his way. Once more it was deadlock.

In October General Sir Charles Monro, who had replaced the ineffectual Hamilton, urged that the Gallipoli campaign be abandoned. Lord Kitchener, the British war figurehead, visited the scenes of suffering and reluctantly admitted there was no alternative but withdrawal. His influence and credibility were diminished in London, however, and still politicians wrangled. It was the appointment of Sir William Robertson which decided the matter. The general, who had risen through the ranks, was respected by war-time prime minister Herbert Henry Asquith; he favoured France as the theatre of war. He declared the government should end the sideshow in Gallipoli.

In December 1915 the bulk of the troops was evacuated, with complete success. Not a shot was fired.

In eight months the British and Australasian forces, some 500,000 strong, had notched up 252,000 casualties and gained nothing. For the Turks the dead and wounded numbered 251,000.

The fiasco reflected badly on Winston Churchill, innovator of the plan, who could scarcely believe how badly it had been executed. He resigned in fury and frustration. But the commanders responsible for the carnage throughout the war escaped without even a reprimand.

Above: *British troops in Gallipoli had little idea what they were fighting for. Only later did they discover the hopelessness of their cause.*

ROBERT MAXWELL
Robbing the poor to feed the rich

In World War 2 Robert Maxwell won the Military Cross for bravery and was honoured as a hero. After his death thousands of pensioners cursed him as a crook.

On Guy Fawkes Night 1991 Captain Gus Rankin, master of the luxury yacht *Lady Ghislaine*, radioed an emergency message that sent shockwaves through the world's corridors of power. The Publisher was missing, feared dead, off the Canary Islands. He had apparently slipped into the water while the vessel was cruising, and drowned.

Robert Maxwell had been best known as a self-important, publicity-seeking bully. Above all, he was obsessively vain. However, predictably, when any well-known figure dies the fulsome tributes come flooding in and Maxwell's passing proved no exception.

Former prime minister Margaret Thatcher spoke of the valuable information on Eastern Europe he would pass to her, her predecessor Edward Heath praised Maxwell's unstinting support for the European ideal, Neil Kinnock talked of his backing for the Labour Party in glowing terms, while John Major observed

that Maxwell would not want the world to grieve at his death but marvel at his extraordinary life. Even Mikhail Gorbachev chipped in with a piece of gibberish acknowledging Maxwell's enormous contribution to understanding between nations in mass-media management.

Gorbachev's words, as it turned out, could hardly have been further from the truth. For as the Maxwell family prepared for the great man's burial on the Mount of Olives in Israel, bankers, accountants and financiers quietly began to assess their exposure to Maxwell's business borrowings. They did not like what they saw. The bonfire of the vanities was about to begin.

A HOUSE OF CARDS

Within days the first hint of a monumental financial scandal was starting to creep out. Many in the City, together with most of the better-informed financial journalists, had known for years that the flagship company, Maxwell Communications Corporation, was heavily borrowed with comparatively few hard assets. It was a house of cards. Maxwell's death would bring it tumbling down.

Much of the empire was so complicated, with a worldwide web of interlinked companies and trusts, that no one except Maxwell himself understood how it worked. He had been careful to shelter much of his business away from prying eyes in discreet havens such as Liechtenstein and the Cayman Islands, where enquiries about financial matters – official or otherwise – tended to hit brick walls. Whenever he raided the coffers of his companies, cash left unspent would end up offshore.

Above: *Family mourners await the funeral on Israel's Mount of Olives. Lifting the coffin was a feat in itself.*

Opposite: *Maxwell, a self-important, publicity-mad bully. Only he understood the complexities of his world-wide business empire.*

Below left: *With Margaret Thatcher. He passed her valuable information on Eastern European countries.*

Below: *Maxwell House, HQ of Maxwell Communications Corporation.*

MAXWELL HOUSE

PENSIONERS WOKE UP TO
DISCOVER THAT THE FUNDS
THAT THEY HAD DEPENDED
ON FOR THEIR OLD AGE HAD
BEEN FRITTERED AWAY.

Below: Mirror *pensioners on the march after finding that their nest-eggs had been plundered.*

But one criminal fact already shone out like a warning beacon. Maxwell had clearly plundered millions from the pension fund of his favourite company, Mirror Group Newspapers. The estimates varied but the £400 million the experts calculated seemed about right. Word spread like lightning and politicians and the media turned on Maxwell with a vengeance. Even his own paper, the *Daily Mirror*, denounced him with righteous indignation as a fraud and a crook.

of a free, fearless press? Why wasn't the charlatan exposed?

Firstly, because he was notoriously litigious. Writs from Maxwell, it was said, could fly out faster than his presses could print. He seemed to relish the prospect of cowing his enemies in the courts and legal costs were irrelevant to him. In the knowledge that Britain's laws of libel were among the most oppressive in the world, and with the recession slicing into their profits, the newspapermen stayed ominously silent.

If the merest hint of a rumour defamatory of Maxwell came to his attention he would instruct his lawyers to send a curt note to every editor in Fleet Street. They would run the story at their peril.

But it wasn't only legal bluster that restrained the papers. Before his death and subsequent unmasking, Maxwell was seen as the Man Who Got Things Done. He was a World War 2 hero, champion of the world's starving, a former Labour MP and an entrepreneur who genuinely could count many of the world's monarchs, emperors, dictators, presidents and prime ministers as his close confidante. In short, he was hot on influence. His friends in high places could always oblige with a quiet word in the ear of a journalist who was sniffing a bit too close to a Maxwell scoop.

Below: *With Prince Charles and Prince William.*

The vitriol was undeniably justified. Thousands of *Mirror* employees and pensioners literally woke up one morning to discover their pot of cash, which for some had taken 40 years to build up, had been frittered away by Maxwell in an attempt to keep his companies afloat during the cold recessionary years of the 1980s.

They guessed – and they were probably right – that the money went on a futile share support operation to try to prop up the London Stock Exchange price of MCC. The reason was simple: Maxwell used shares from his businesses as collateral to borrow more cash from the banks. The banks were happy as long as the businesses flourished but when share prices began plummeting so did the value of their security. In the months before his death they were getting more and more edgy and pressure mounted on Chairman Robert.

So why did those in the know stay silent? What happened to the great British tradition

'THE BOUNCING CZECH'

And John Major was right about his extraordinary past. Almost from the day he was born, 10 June 1923, a Czechoslovakian of Jewish parents, his life was one long roller-coaster. Not for nothing was he nicknamed the 'Bouncing Czech'.

Maxwell was born Jan Ludwig Hoch in one of the poorest parts of Czechoslovakia. At 5 years old he assured his father, a farm labourer: 'When I'm older I will own a cow and a field and make my own living.' The peasants who had to mount a daily fight against starvation laughed out loud at such a ridiculous suggestion.

It seemed even less likely the following year when young Jan caught diphtheria – then an often fatal disease. There were fears that he would never fully recover; never become strong enough to earn a living on his own. As he would do so often in his life, he contemptuously swept aside the doubters and got on with fulfilling his dreams.

At 12 he walked an incredible 400 miles from his home village of Solotvino to the city of Bratislava to look for work. Later, he laughed off the achievement, saying: 'If I were a woman I would always be pregnant. I never can say no to a challenge.'

His war record bore out that claim. He started out as a Czech soldier in Central Europe where the Nazi atrocities he encountered left him with a burning hatred of Hitler. At one stage he tried to join the French Foreign Legion, lying about his age in order to qualify, but as Hitler's hordes swept across Europe, he found himself evacuated by the Royal Navy and ended up in Liverpool. From now on his determination to defeat the Nazis took a new edge. All his family, apart from two sisters, had become victims of the Holocaust.

Maxwell wangled his way into the British Army as Private J.L. Hoch, serial number 12079140. He fought with enormous skill and courage and was decorated with the Military Cross – one of the highest honours in the army – after leading his platoon against a German pillbox in Brussels in 1944. Later he would waste no opportunity to retell his war stories. One of his Mirror Group editors revealed: 'He told me of one time at the end of the war when he was in France. He went into a barn and found a German soldier who was about 15. He told Maxwell to put up his arms and surrender. Maxwell told him to drop his gun in German. The boy did. I asked Maxwell what he did then. "I shot him, of course, you bloody fool," he replied, smiling.'

The war over, he set about building a career in publishing. Wary of any lingering Jewish hatred in Europe, he adopted the very British-sounding name of Robert Maxwell. He spoke English superbly (he had mastered nine languages by his death) and used his British contacts, such as they were, to the full. But it was only after establishing a niche in scientific publishing and distribution in

Left: *Lieutenant Robert Maxwell MC leads his men during the Victory Parade through Berlin in September 1945.*

Opposite bottom right: *A youthful Maxwell in pensive mood as he waits to take his seat as MP for Buckingham.*

Below: *In happier times, Maxwell waves to his investors at a meeting of Pergamum shareholders.*

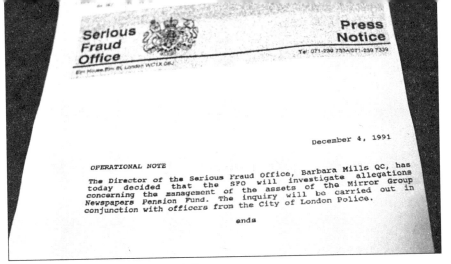

Above: *The Serious Fraud Office announces it is beginning a full investigation into Maxwell's various dealings.*

HE TOLD THE STARVING PEOPLE THAT HE WOULD SAVE THEM. IT WAS JUST ANOTHER OF HIS LIES.

Germany that he spotted the hole in the market which would make his name.

Convinced that cheap scientific textbooks were in demand he used his £300 war gratuity to set up Pergamon Press. The company prospered into a £6 million multinational enterprise and for most of the fifties and sixties Maxwell's wealth and reputation grew steadily higher. Then, in 1969, the bubble burst. Maxwell had agreed to sell Pergamon to a New York financier, who then tried to wriggle out of the deal by claiming there were irregularities in the accounts. The American was right. In a bloody internal battle Maxwell was sacked by his own board and vilified in a government investigation. The Department of Trade concluded he was not a fit person to run a public company.

Yet within five years he had bounced back. He regained control of Pergamon and began expanding his horizons with a vengeance. By the beginning of the eighties he controlled the British Printing Corporation and prepared to set up the single biggest European printing group. Cash for the deal came largely from the National Westminster, and with typical Maxwell nerve he called the bank's chairman with a plan to print all their cheque books. 'After all,' he boomed, 'you and I have a mutual interest in doing business together.'

In 1984 he seized control of Mirror Group Newspapers and immediately began restructuring an organization dogged by inept management practices. Because print unions then dictated their own manpower levels, MGN had been paying printers whether there was a job for them or not. As a result some 'inkies' would clock on for a shift under the name Mickey Mouse, or some equally absurd pseudonym. Then they'd trot off to do another job secure in the knowledge that no one at the newspaper would be checking to see where they were.

BONFIRE OF VANITIES

The print unions were then perhaps the most powerful in Britain. In Maxwell, though, they met their match. He modernized the presses and introduced new technology and full colour printing. Sackings were frequent but the paper slowly began to look better and better. The only embarrassing snag for its journalists was their chairman's desire to have stories constantly appearing about his own wonderful deeds.

The classic example was his decision to launch a mercy mission for the starving of Ethiopia in 1984. He persuaded British Airways' Lord King to lend him a Tristar to carry supplies, a readers' appeal fund was launched and the paper carried columns and columns of stories about the way Maxwell was opening doors which had long stayed closed through British government bureaucracy. One former employee recalled a typical early morning meeting at which Maxwell would issue orders in the manner of a general stalking his war room.

'Get me Lord Sainsbury on the phone at home. And the chairman of Boots. And those people who promised us the milk powder. I don't give a damn if this is Sunday morning. Tell them it's a matter of life and death.'

His arrival in Addis Ababa was like a scene from a Carry On film. Maxwell strode into the airport sweeping aside immigration officials and flashing withering stares at anyone in uniform who dared to enter into his presence. Behind him a so-called welcoming party trotted along meekly in a mixture of bafflement and excitement. Then he faced the assembled ranks of press, TV, and radio, sporting his blue John Lennon-style cap and wearing his best Churchillian demeanour.

'There have been complaints that Western aid to Ethiopia is too little, too late,' he boomed. 'Well, speaking on behalf of the British nation I dispute that.' No one ventured to ask how he obtained the authority to speak for Britain. Anyway, there wasn't time. Turning on his heels Maxwell was already heading for a group of Ethiopian government dignitaries. Grabbing the hand of the nearest minister he looked him straight in the eye and declared: 'Things are going to be very different for your country from now on. Kindly tell the president that Robert Maxwell is here.'

BULLYING

When not fighting battles abroad, Maxwell loved nothing better than a chance to torment his editors and senior executives. He would keep them waiting for hours outside his office in Maxwell House, London, while he chattered away to his subordinates around the world or called some nation's leader to offer the benefit of his advice. There were only a couple of seats and a cold water machine in the waiting room.

When they did get summoned into his lair the atmosphere would be electric. Maxwell would often pick out one individual for ritual humiliation in front of his colleagues. One personnel manager was torn to shreds because of a circular letter he had sent to all Pergamon employees. Maxwell claimed: 'My old grandmother, who could never speak a word of English, brought up in the mountains of Carpathia could write better English than this.' He then ordered the unfortunate executive to shuffle out into a side office and write down why he shouldn't be sacked. As he left Maxwell roared with glee at the effects of his bullying.

Maxwell employees were not the only ones who had to bow to his whims. He disliked going out of the office for anyone, preferring them to come to him. Visiting foreign dignitaries would find themselves transported to Maxwell House by Rolls or helicopter from Heathrow. And if a guest was particularly favoured Maxwell would send his Gulfstream jet anywhere in the world.

Occasionally such lavish entertaining turned to farce. Maxwell would simultaneously host dinner for a couple of Japanese businessmen, a buffet lunch for a US trade delegation, a reception for a party of Hungarian newspapermen and plan his own quiet lunch in his study. He would tour from room to room, engaging in conversation, charming any women present, espousing his views on the world but always making an excuse to move on. And, of course, none of his guests was ever aware of the existence of others.

His family (he and his wife Betty had seven children) learned to their cost that business was never separated from home life. The two sons with closest links to the business, Kevin and Ian, were expected to be at work for 7.30 am and could expect a huge dressing down if they were late. They rarely escaped home before a full 12 hours at their desks.

John Pole, Maxwell's head of security since 1986, said: 'He would go home to celebrate Christmas and be bored by Boxing Day. The family would gather for what they thought was going to be a holiday only to find they were going to work, but in a different country. He treated them like employees. Gradually they needed to look to other things to maintain sanity and some family life of their own.'

Top: *Maxwell and his wife Betty, pictured in 1974.*

Above: *Sons Kevin and Ian found themselves embroiled in the SFO investigation.*

Above: *Maxwell in one of his definitive pompous poses. Editors at the Mirror Group hated his thirst for self-publicity.*

Right: *His yacht the* **Lady Ghislaine,** *on which Maxwell spent his last minutes alive. It was among the most luxurious ever built and kept the publisher in touch with his minions via fax machines and satellite phones.*

Vanity was one of Maxwell's biggest vices. He needed to impress – especially women – and he hated the thought that his good looks and once enviable build had gone. Such fears caused him to suffer from bizarre eating disorders. He would suffer from uncontrollable binges, stuffing sandwiches into his mouth at the rate of five or six a time, and then a week later attempt to sustain a hopeless diet of coffee and soup. It did little to affect his usual bulk of 310 lb.

His hair was another obsession. He used to employ a former Savoy Hotel hairdresser, George Wheeler, to colour it for him every two weeks. Maxwell and the crimper would lock themselves away for two hours while the dyes were applied to both hair and eyebrows. Everything was done in secret. No one was supposed to know it happened.

It was the same with his powder puff. Maxwell convinced himself his nose was too shiny so he took powder everywhere with him to counter the effect. If he ever forgot his puff before an important meeting it would throw him into a minor panic. Everything and everyone would have to wait while he went to fetch it. One of his editors, the *Mirror*'s Mike Molloy, recalled: 'Maxwell was theatre, he was looking for an image.'

Only on the *Lady Ghislaine*, named after his favourite daughter, could Maxwell hope to unwind amid the trappings of absolute luxury and forget about crafting that image. He loved nothing better than to sunbathe on his private deck alone, smothering his bloated mass in suncream and sleeping. The yacht was his fortress, his haven, yet at the flick of a switch he could be talking to his minions anywhere in the world by fax or radiophone. The dummy pages of the *Mirror* would regularly be faxed to him for approval.

According to the paper's former foreign editor, Nicholas Davies, who became as close to Maxwell as any newspaperman, sailing on the *Lady Ghislaine* did nothing to quell his bullying habits. Davies recalls: 'On one occasion, after a very good lunch, he phoned his chief of staff, Peter Jay, in Holborn only to find he was out to lunch.

When Jay returned his call, Maxwell turned up the heat demanding to know why he had the temerity to leave the office without permission when the chairman was abroad.

'He demanded Jay write an explanation immediately giving reasons for his absence and fax it to him on the yacht. When he received Jay's long explanatory note Maxwell read it, roaring with laughter, at what he saw as a huge joke. Then he phoned Jay back and tore into him again, pretending to be furious.'

Jay, who eventually resigned to pursue a career as economics editor with the BBC, would later tell of the 'whirling chaos' that surrounded Maxwell's operations. It was this lack of structure that meant no one but Maxwell knew the whole truth about his affairs. At times he must have struggled himself.

Jay said: 'He was not just disorderly, he actively abhorred order. The key to the man was that he had the lowest threshold of boredom. He would come in and say: "What shall I do?" He'd get an idea and start ringing people. They would turn up and wait to be told what to do, by which time he would be on to something else ... from grotesque schemes for transforming the world to fantastic rows about running newspapers.'

In a note to his successor Jay acidly observed: 'The job is essentially administration, a process of which the chairman is deeply suspicious and profoundly uncomprehending.'

PARANOID

Even when he was aboard the *Lady Ghislaine*, though, Maxwell could never truly relax. In his last years he became increasingly paranoid about the risk of attack, seeing himself as particularly vulnerable while on the yacht. He had one of his early captains, Englishman Mike Insull, buy an armoury equipped with guns for every member of crew. They were sent on courses to learn how to use them in the event of a boarding by raiders. But the guns were never referred to by name. Maxwell called them vegetables, and at the start of a voyage would sometimes sidle up to Insull and ask 'How many carrots and potatoes have you brought on this trip?'

Inevitably, after such a bizarre death, there was talk that Maxwell did not just slip into the sea by accident. Some remain convinced

he committed suicide, broken by the knowledge that his entire business empire was only weeks away from crashing around his ears. Others talk of an Arab assassin hired to wipe out a man they considered an agent for the Mossad, the Israeli secret service. Another, even more outlandish, claim is that he was rubbed out by the Mafia for trying to break into their lucrative stranglehold on US newspapers. Finally, it is rumoured the remains of the Soviet KGB had decided to settle an old score.

Of the four, the suicide theory, argue old Maxwell acquaintances, is the hardest to accept. Nicholas Davies tells how only once in the years he knew Maxwell did he hear him refer directly to suicide. Davies had been summoned to his boss's London apartment to talk over the debut of the

OUTLANDISH CLAIMS CIRCULATED AFTER HIS DEATH: ARAB ASSASSINS, THE KGB AND THE MAFIA WERE ACCUSED OF HIS MURDER.

European, his new weekly broadsheet paper. Maxwell appeared dispirited and had a heavy cold. He lounged on his bed in a white towelling robe making dismissive remarks about the paper. Then he walked to the window overlooking the city and began talking, half to himself.

'Sometimes I don't know why I go on. Everything I try, people turn against me ... I've got no friends, no one I can talk to ... no one to share my life with ... Sometimes I think I should just end it all, throw myself out of the window. I sometimes feel I can't go on.'

It was one of the few occasions anyone ever heard Maxwell admit to the failure of

Above: *Ever the extrovert, Maxwell cracks jokes with fellow party guests Liz Taylor and Malcolm Forbes. He loved nothing better than rubbing shoulders with world leaders or film stars.*

his personal life. Perhaps he now knew his business empire was teetering on the edge of ruin as well. Had he stared into the abyss and realized what lay ahead? In his own mind, had he made a decision to end his life? If so, he picked the most theatrical way out possible. Disappearing from a yacht as it cruised the waters of the Canaries would, he

Above: *The auction of fittings from Maxwell's London penthouse was billed as the sale of the century.*

Below: *Kevin Maxwell leaving court.*

knew, guarantee even more column inches on the story of his demise.

The Arab attack theory is intriguing and if it sounds fanciful it should be taken in context with the rest of Maxwell's life. Everything that happened to him had the whiff of pure fiction. Just two weeks before

his death, the respected US Pulitzer Prize-winning author, Seymour Hersh, made extraordinary allegations in his book *The Samson Option*. Maxwell, he said, had for years been a Mossad agent who specialized in negotiating arms deals for Israel. But why should Maxwell bother with Mossad when he was on first-name terms with their own masters in the Israeli cabinet? And why, if Arab terrorists were responsible, did no credible organization claim responsibility?

The KGB conspiracy theory is neat and just about believable, but with Russia in a state of enormous upheaval at the time surely Red spy controllers had more important issues to tackle than killing a fat entrepreneur out on a sailing jaunt? It is said that for years Maxwell had been laundering US dollars for the Russians, taking a cut for his trouble and tucking away the proceeds in his Maxwell Foundation trust in Liechtenstein. He had also looked after the wealth of some senior Communist party figures who wanted to get their money out of the country in the face of an imminent counter-revolution.

With Russia on the brink of civil war, so the theory goes, KGB spymasters decided it was time to call in their debts. They reckoned Maxwell had made millions on the back of their cash, playing the foreign exchange markets with his natural gambler's instincts. The amounts were said to run into tens of millions of dollars and when Maxwell failed to take up the KGB's 'invitation' to pay their dividend there was talk of double-crossing. It was then that the KGB decided to show they could still flex their muscles and an agent somehow sneaked aboard the *Lady Ghislaine* to tip Maxwell over the side.

MURDER BY THE MOB?

Finally, of course, there's the mob theory. In February 1991 Maxwell had taken over the New York *Daily News* in a blaze of publicity. With a beaming face, and sporting a *Daily News* baseball cap, he gleefully held up the front page of his new baby bearing the headline: 'Roll 'em – hats off to Maxwell as News gets bigger & better than ever'.

Not everyone was happy. There were persistent rumours that for years the *News*'s distribution network had been in the hands of an organized crime syndicate. Maxwell, however, knew the Mafia men were on the

run following a police crackdown. He reckoned the only barrier to introducing new technology and making the paper profitable was the intransigent unions.

Maxwell took one of his top aides into negotiations with the unions. Scotsman Ian Watson, then a senior executive with the *European*, was tasked with trying to persuade them to accept redundancies and economies. Watson later revealed: 'After seven of the ten print unions had agreed to the cutbacks, I went to see the leaders of the remaining three, who were holding out. I remember most vividly the conversation I had with one union official. He said to me, in a broad Brooklyn accent, "Are you a New Yorker? Do you know New Yorkers? Do you understand them? If you think you can push us into an agreement you'll end up in the East River with your throats slit. All of you."' Watson said later: 'He wasn't playacting. He was deadly serious.'

Maxwell took no chances. Firstly, he asked the Manhattan district attorney's office to conduct an inquiry into the organized crime allegations. Secondly, he decided he ought to get personal protection – those who met him whenever he was in New York said he seemed to be more and more preoccupied. So it was that only days before his death he held a meeting with the head of America's most respected private security firm, Jules Kroll of Kroll Associates.

Maxwell's full conversations with Kroll have never been made public, but those close to him, such as Nicholas Davies, believe Maxwell made it clear that people were out to kill him and destroy his businesses. He named names – business rivals, known enemies and political adversaries. At the end of their two-hour talk Kroll told him to set down a memo listing the bizarre events which had led him to draw this conclusion. He never did pen that memo for within a week he had drowned.

There is, of course, the other possibility, the theory that doesn't make headlines or attract TV documentary makers. This holds that Maxwell got drunk (as he often did, especially on the yacht where Dom Perignon was always available on ice) and took a walk round the decks in the early hours because he felt unwell. Certainly his crew recall him radioing through to complain about the air conditioning. Did he just slip over a low rail close to the waterline, as some have

suggested? If so, his cries for help would fall on deaf ears. None of the crew would have been on deck at the time and the speed of the yacht would have quickly carried her away from the drowning Maxwell's spluttering cries.

Whatever the truth, it matters little to the 30,000 *Mirror* pensioners who have endured agonies wondering how they will attain the retirement life-style they planned so carefully. Legal arguments about the Maxwell empire seem certain to rage on well into the next millennium. As for Maxwell himself, a hundred epitaphs could never tell his story of courage, meteoric rise, fraud and ultimate failure. All you can say is that he died as he lived … bizarrely, mysteriously … and with the newspapers chasing close behind.

Above: *A literary lunch at London's Dorchester Hotel in 1969. Already Maxwell is looking distinctly flabby – his weight became an obsession in later life.*

MAXWELL VOICED HIS FEARS TO THE HEAD OF A POWERFUL PRIVATE SECURITY FIRM; A WEEK LATER HE WAS DEAD.

THE RACE TO THE POLES

The quest for glory has driven men across frozen wastes to the very ends of the Earth, risking all on a gamble. Some win, and have riches and honours heaped upon them. And some lose ...

For years it had been the Holy Grail of seafarers: to find a shorter voyage from western Europe to the Orient, and to open a new trade link through the Arctic with all the profits that it entailed.

The search for a North West Passage had ended in failure many times, yet to explorers like Sir John Franklin that record served only as an added spur. If any nation was to find this elusive route it should, he felt, be his native Britain. Wasn't she the greatest naval power on Earth? Didn't her seamen have unrivalled experience? And, surely, her ships were the best?

On 19 May 1845 Sir John's expedition set sail with two ships, the *Erebus* and the *Terror*. Both had proved themselves more than capable of coping with icy seas (they had been used on an earlier jaunt by James Clark Ross to the South Pole) and they were stocked with enough carefully preserved provisions to last a good three years.

The Franklin party left in a fanfare of publicity with newspapers recording intimate details of the dangerous journey ahead. Nobody believed the voyage would be easy, but in the highest ranks of the Admiralty, and government itself, there was a quiet confidence that Sir John would somehow navigate his way through the labyrinth of straits, narrow channels and rocky gulfs known to lie in his way.

AN OMINOUS SILENCE

After two years, however, with no word from either *Erebus* or *Terror*, public opinion began to show signs of concern. Of course, the crews couldn't yet be out of food or water but all the same it seemed an ominous silence. Throughout the bitter British winter of 1847–48 tension grew. The government had to be seen to be doing something in the face of mounting pressure, and after enlisting the help of the Hudson's Bay Company, who in turn alerted roaming bands of Eskimos out on the Arctic wastes, they offered a reward of £20,000 which they hoped would help track Franklin down.

It didn't. By the summer of 1848 plans for a full-scale British search and rescue mission were well under way. Two vessels would scour known North West Passage sea lanes around the Bering Strait, while a land party would head north from Canada. Another group, headed by the acclaimed explorer James Ross, would push into the Arctic region from the east.

That winter Ross and his crew landed on Somerset Island – thought to have been a

Above: *Sir John Franklin. His attempt to navigate the North West Passage turned into a disaster.*

Opposite: *Robert Falcon Scott, a ruthless taskmaster and disciplinarian – yet he would hide when a sled dog had to be destroyed, leaving the job to his men.*

Above: *Franklin at Bear Lake. He believed passionately that British ships should be the first through the North West Passage.*

THE MUTILATED STATE OF THE BODIES INDICATED THAT THE DYING MEN HAD TRIED TO SURVIVE BY EATING HUMAN FLESH.

Right: *Austin's* **Expedition,** *one of the many ships sent to search for Franklin. The three largest from the left are* **Assistance, Resolute** *and* **Pioneer. Intrepid** *is slightly to the left of* **Assistance.**

possible staging post for Franklin – and covered 200 miles looking for him. They drew a blank and when they returned to England empty-handed it was seen by many as a certain sign of the Franklin party's death. Yet the Admiralty was nothing if not persistent and the following year a wave of 15 new search parties, carrying hundreds of would-be rescuers, set sail for the Arctic.

Among them was a nine-ship fleet commanded by Captain Horatio Austin with orders to search the Barrow Straits thoroughly. Austin came upon a god-forsaken, largely uninhabitable piece of land called Beechey Island and, true to his brief, decided to check it out. One of his officers, Captain Ommaney of HMS *Assistance*, took a search party ashore and with keen eyes carefully scanned the forbidding landscape.

Suddenly his eyes caught something odd: order amid the chaos, a symmetrical object in a sea of random rocks and scrub. When he got to it he found it was a primitive forge, a

store and what appeared to be a shooting gallery. There were hundreds of cans of meat stacked up ready to eat and, nearby, tombs bearing the names of three of Franklin's men. But what fate had befallen the others?

In 1853 Dr John Rae, an official with the Hudson's Bay Company, provided at least part of the answer. He had set out to cover the area around the Gulf of Boothia, an area where Eskimos were known to congregate as they waited to send hunting parties out onto the Arctic ice. Sure enough the Eskimos handed him a gigantic clue. Some other Eskimos, they said, had reported meeting a demoralized party of 40 white men who were travelling south to a point about 150 miles from where Rae now stood.

CANNIBALISM

The strangers had abandoned two large ships and claimed they were heading for the Back River. Many in their party appeared to be suffering from exhaustion and scurvy ... but at least Rae now knew there might be some survivors. Some Eskimos even claimed to have boarded the *Erebus* and the *Terror* off the coast of King William Island. Others offered grimmer news: they had stumbled upon the graves of some 30 men close to the Back River. Many of the bodies had lain huddled together in tents; others were found sheltering under a boat.

It must have been an appalling way to die, for as Rae noted after visiting the doomed camp: 'From the mutilated state of many of the bodies, and the contents of the kettles, it is evident

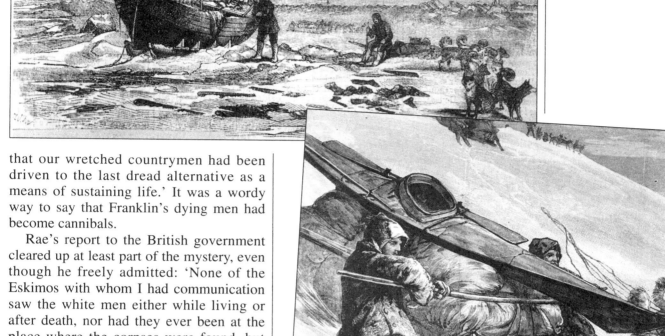

that our wretched countrymen had been driven to the last dread alternative as a means of sustaining life.' It was a wordy way to say that Franklin's dying men had become cannibals.

Rae's report to the British government cleared up at least part of the mystery, even though he freely admitted: 'None of the Eskimos with whom I had communication saw the white men either while living or after death, nor had they ever been at the place where the corpses were found, but had their information from natives who had been there.' Despite this the government handed over half the reward money in recognition of Rae's fearless investigations. It then declared the search over, mainly on the grounds that the cost of finding 100 men (possibly scattered widely across the Arctic) was impractical. Lady Franklin's plea for a new seafarer to take up the challenge was firmly rejected.

It made little difference to her. She was not a woman easily dissuaded by anyone and with the man she loved now missing for more than seven years she set herself on raising the money for a privately funded expedition. Influential friends rallied round and on 1 July 1857 a compact steamer called the *Fox* slipped her moorings at Aberdeen and under the command of one Leopold McClintock – a veteran of previous searches – headed for the Arctic.

After stopping to take on sledge dogs and an Eskimo interpreter in Greenland the *Fox* made for Lancaster Sound. The aim was to find a suitable mooring point from which to launch a land-based search. Unfortunately massive quantities of drift ice left the ship totally immobile and she was forced to drift aimlessly with the current for an agonizing 242 days … in the wrong direction. It was not until 1 March 1859 that McClintock unearthed his first

solid clue as to the fate of Franklin's men.

He was leading a small land party across the Boothia Peninsula when they met a group of Eskimo hunters. With help from his interpreter McClintock learned that years earlier a large ship had been crushed by ice off King William Island. All the crew had escaped, they believed, but then headed for a great river where they succumbed to the cold

It seemed to confirm Rae's discoveries and McClintock made haste back to his ship. His destination now was King William Island and the Back River and he divided his men into two with the intention of searching as thoroughly as possible.

On the island yet more hard clues emerged. Some Eskimos showed off items of silverware stamped with the crests of Franklin and his brother officers. Yet when McClintock at last reached the waters of the Back River he was disappointed. There were no signs of any crude settlement; no trace of white men whatsoever.

Above left: *The boat around which 30 of Franklin's men fought – and lost – their battle for survival. Some had resorted to cannibalism.*

Above: *An artist's impression of how Franklin's men would have struggled to cross the polar ice-fields.*

Above: *Lieutenant Hobson's party breaks open the cairn at Point Victory. Inside were records telling them how* **Terror** *and* **Erebus** *had been abandoned after two years locked in ice.*

Right: *Roald Amundsen. He walked away from a medical career to become an explorer.*

THE FINAL CLUES

The party crossed back to King William Island and headed up the west coast in an attempt to link up with the *Fox*'s other search party. Then, at last, they got the break they had been praying for. A weather-battered skeleton still dressed in the tatty remnants of European clothes was found lying on a snow-covered beach. On the body McClintock found a small pocket book containing a handful of letters – but still no formal record of the expedition's fate.

A little further on the searchers found two more skeletons, this time lying in a 28-foot-long boat which seemed to have once come from a ship. There were a couple of watches, two guns, spare clothing and tea and chocolate ... but still no paper records. In a further baffling twist, the boat faced north. Franklin's men could have been expected to flee south from the wrecks of their ships. Did the two unfortunates in the boat make a last desperate bid to turn back for the safety of the *Erebus* and *Terror*? If so, they had badly over-estimated their chances.

Instinct told McClintock to head north. His own log describes succinctly what happened next.

'A few miles beyond Cape Herschel the land becomes very low; many islets and shingle ridges lie far off the coast; and as we advanced we met hummocks of unusually heavy ice ... we were approaching a spot where a revelation of intense interest was awaiting.

'About 12 miles from Cape Herschel I found a small cairn built by Hobson's search party [Lieutenant Hobson was one of the *Fox*'s senior officers] and containing a note for me.'

Hobson it was who, on 6 May 1859, finally uncovered the secret of Franklin's doomed party. At Point Victory, on the north-west coast of King William Island, he found a large cairn surrounded by piles of equipment such as stoves, pickaxes, canvas shovels and instruments. There was also a rusty old cylinder which appeared to have been opened and then re-soldered. Inside they found two independently dated notices.

One log told how the *Terror* and *Erebus* had finally been abandoned on 22 April 1848 after more than two years trapped in the ice. Signed Captain F.R.M. Crozier, it ended with the postscript: 'start tomorrow, 26th, for Back's Great River'.

McClintock's men may have found the

last traces of the ill-fated Franklin expedition but they failed to answer the most important questions of all. Where did Franklin himself die? Why didn't his men join the Eskimos and learn their survival skills? And why had he been forced away from Back River? The answers remain largely conjecture.

The tragedy of Franklin's failure had, by now, been largely forgotten back home in Britain. It had certainly not dissuaded other explorers from pursuing the dream of conquering the elusive North West Passage.

A GLITTERING CHALLENGE

Foremost among them was a young Norwegian called Roald Amundsen. He was born in 1872, 13 years after the last hopes of finding Franklin had expired, yet throughout his boyhood he had nurtured an ambition to succeed where the Englishman had failed.

Although he had been channelled into a medical career the 21-year-old Amundsen decided to follow the instincts of his heart rather than his head. He threw up his studies to prepare for a career as an explorer, starting as a seaman aboard an Arctic merchantman and later serving as first mate aboard the *Belgica*, the first vessel to winter in the Antarctic.

On returning to Norway Amundsen decided to mount his own North West Passage expedition. He purchased a sturdy 72-foot ship called the *Gjoa* and during a series of voyages between 1903 and 1906 became the first man to navigate the route successfully. A glittering future now beckoned, with Amundsen a household name around the world and a hero at home. Instead of basking in the fame, the Norwegian immediately began planning his next challenge ... conquering the North Pole.

Amundsen's plans were to drift across it in a ship, a technique pioneered by his countryman Fridtjof Nansen in 1893. Nansen had noticed that wood used by Greenlanders was not from any indigenous tree population. Botanists reported that rough driftwood cast up on the shores originated from as far away as Siberia: it could only have travelled in a current which passed over the roof of the world.

Nansen's brave attempt to drift with the pack ice across the Pole had been technically

a failure, though he did get to within 272 miles of the Pole. His expedition lasted more than three years and he was given up for lost in Norway after setting out from his ship, the *Fram*, with one of his young officers, Hjalmar Johansen. In the summer of 1896 the exhausted pair stumbled onto a group of desolate islands called Frans Josef Land. Miraculously they there ran into an English explorer called Frederick Jackson, who at first refused to believe what he was seeing.

Finally Jackson ventured: 'Aren't you Nansen?' The man nodded, Jackson grabbed his hand and with typical British understatement told him: 'By Jove, I am glad to see you.'

Amundsen was convinced he could make Nansen's drift theory work but sadly never got the chance. Money was tight in his government's coffers and his expedition was still in the early stages of preparation when, in September 1909, news flashed around the globe that American naval officer Robert E. Peary had conquered the North Pole.

Cannily, Amundsen hid his disappointment and announced he would continue with plans for an Arctic 'drift'. In fact his motives were almost certainly very different. He was little over a year away from one of the greatest pieces of real-life drama in the history of man's exploration of the Earth.

Above: *Nansen meets Jackson after more than three years lost in the polar wastes.*

Below: *Admiral Peary. He beat Scott and Amundsen in the race to the North Pole.*

Right: *Roald Amundsen. He was first to the South Pole, through meticulous planning, wide experience and sheer single-mindedness.*

Below: Terra Nova *at anchor near Cape Evans, Antarctica.*

SCOTT OF THE ANTARCTIC

That same year the Englishman Robert Scott, already a veteran of Antarctic campaigns, announced his ambition to conquer the South Pole. He chose an old whaling ship, the *Terra Nova*, and made plans to take a party of scientists with him. They would travel on sledges pulled by Manchurian ponies (Scott had been less than impressed with the efforts of dogs on his earlier expeditions).

Scott hardly seemed the ideal character to lead such a taxing adventure. When he was a naval cadet his lecturers regarded him as unashamedly lazy, somewhat slovenly and prone to bouts of extraordinary temper. Later in his career he was marked out as a ruthless taskmaster and stickler for discipline. Yet he inspired faith and respect among his men, perhaps because despite his weak chest and comparatively puny physique he drove himself far harder than he drove them.

Scott was also something of a romantic. His day-dreaming earned him the nickname 'old mooney' and he had a habit of crying when he heard certain hymns. He hated anything he regarded as cruel and hid himself away if it was ever necessary to put down a sled dog. Though he had the heart of a lion and unrivalled willpower, his failing was to lack Amundsen's more practical, direct approach to problems.

On 1 June 1910 the *Terra Nova* set sail from the Port of London bound for New

Zealand. A couple of months later Amundsen, using Nansen's proven vessel the *Fram*, also headed south with the apparent intention of rounding Cape Horn to take the Pacific route up to the North Pole. His entire crew believed the Arctic was their destination.

On 9 September at Funchal in the Madeira Islands, Amundsen dropped his bombshell. Far from heading north, he said, they would press south. Their mission was to conquer the South Pole and anyone who didn't wish to proceed was free to leave. Unsurprisingly there were no takers. Scott had not yet reached Melbourne, Australia, but when he did there was a succinctly phrased cable waiting for him. It was from Madeira and read: 'BEG LEAVE TO INFORM YOU PROCEEDING ANTARCTICA STOP AMUNDSEN'.

The news was greeted first with incredulity, then indignation by members of the British team. They had been pitched into a race for which they had never been mentally prepared, but if that was the way Amundsen wanted it, so be it.

Scott made haste for his base camp on McMurdo Sound, on the far east of the Ross Ice Shelf, but found the going through pack ice extremely slow. While waiting for the camp to be resupplied he sailed further east to spy out the lie of the land. In the Bay of Whales his nagging suspicion proved correct. Amundsen's *Fram* already lay rocking gently at anchor. And the

single-mindedness. For a start, his only aim was to reach the Pole as quickly as possible and return safely. Scott would have to make regular stops to allow his scientists to carry out their observations.

Second, the Norwegian had learned from the Eskimos how to dress lightly and warmly in loose-fitting furs to survive polar conditions. His party were better insulated and drier than Scott's men could ever hope to be in their specially constructed suits that weighed almost twice as much and stayed perpetually sodden.

Third, Amundsen's Siberian huskies

Left: *Captain Scott sets out on his last journey. He wore a specially constructed man-made suit – but it quickly became heavy and sodden.*

Norwegian had started out 60 miles nearer the Pole than he would from his base in McMurdo.

Apart from that, Amundsen had won three main advantages through meticulous planning, wide experience and sheer

were excellent performers who had been transported from Greenland under the most carefully controlled conditions possible. All the animals were fit and in perfect shape for the torturous road ahead and they were working for men who knew how to get the best out of them. Each sledge had also been intelligently reduced in weight from the planned 165 lb to a much more manageable 48 lb. Scott, meanwhile, was about to discover that his Manchurian ponies, of whom so much had been made when his expedition left London, were hopeless in extreme snow conditions.

Above: *Manchurian ponies on Scott's expedition. They proved useless in extreme conditions.*

Left: *Amundsen taking a reading with a sextant. His Eskimo-style furs proved far more practical than his rival's gear.*

Above: *Once the ponies had gone, Scott had no choice but to man-haul his sled.*

Below: *Amundsen locating the exact position of the South Pole. He recalled how the Norwegian flag looked 'wonderfully well in the pure clear air'.*

THE RACE FOR GLORY

Amundsen left the Bay of Whales in October with four companions, four sledges, and 52 dogs. They covered 90 miles in the first four days and by 5 November had reached their southernmost supply point ready for the last push to the Pole. Amundsen was then able to strap on skis, attach a rope to a sledge, and have himself towed along. He later admitted: 'Yes, that was a pleasant surprise. We had never dreamed of driving on skis to the Pole.'

By this method the members of the Norwegian team found themselves only 270 miles from their target by the middle of November. Time was overwhelmingly on their side.

Scott, on the other hand, had left McMurdo Sound on 1 November and quickly ran into trouble on the Ross Ice Shelf. An Antarctic summer blizzard meant his ponies began sinking up to their necks in snow and had to be driven to their physical limits by the team. After camping for four days to wait out the storm Scott tried to push forward again. Within 15 hours his few remaining animals had to be shot and his party prepared to manhaul the sledges.

None the less the British kept going, in the clear knowledge that their duel was not only with Amundsen but also with the oncoming grip of winter. They got to their final supply point at the foot of the Beardmore Glacier well behind their planned schedule, but they still believed they could win the race. They now had the broad expanse of the glacier to move across. Amundsen, they reasoned, could not hope for such a straightforward passage.

Amundsen, indeed, had hit his first real snag. He had no choice but to negotiate a narrow ice spur he called the Axel Heiberg glacier and he found the snow so thick and crumbly that the dogs kept losing their footing. Time and again he was forced to retrace his steps to find another way up, and finally, with the way forward blocked by massive slabs of ice, he resigned himself to finding another route south. He still believed he had a good lead on Scott … and he was right.

Several hundred miles away across the unforgiving, icy wastes the British team was showing classic symptoms of fatigue.

They had just lugged their equipment 8,000 feet up the Beardmore Glacier and they remained less than half way to the South Pole.

By 7 December Amundsen had pressed ahead to latitude 88° 23' – 97 miles from the Pole – the farthest point that Irishman Sir Ernest Shackleton had reached the previous year. To commemorate the breaking of Shackleton's record Amundsen ordered the hoisting of the Norwegian national flag on one sledge. In his book *South Pole* he later recalled his thoughts.

'All the sledges had stopped and from the foremost of them the Norwegian flag was flying. It shook itself out, waved and flapped so that the silk rustled; it looked wonderfully well in the pure clear air and the shining, white surroundings … No other moment in the whole trip affected me like this. The tears forced their way to my eyes; by no effort of will could I keep them back. Luckily, I was some way in advance of the others so that I had time to pull myself together and master my feelings before reaching my comrades.'

A week later he was just 15 miles from his goal. Amundsen recalled that he 'had the same feeling that I can remember as a little boy of the night before Christmas Eve – an intense expectation of what was going to happen'.

At 3 pm the next day the magical figure of 90° south was confirmed by the team, though just to be sure they made a 12-mile circuit of the spot, taking further sightings as they went. By general agreement it was decided to leave a tent at the South Pole with the Norwegian flag fluttering from its roof. It would be a sight to chill the heart of Robert Scott.

As Amundsen headed home, Scott's men ploughed on – growing ever wearier from the weight of their sledges. Yet on New Year's Day 1912 their leader entered an optimistic note in his log: 'Only 170 miles to the Pole and plenty of food.' Perhaps it was a touch of over-confidence that caused him on 4 December to make perhaps the greatest mistake of the entire mission.

The last dash beckoned and it had always been agreed that the make-up of this final assault party should be Scott, Captain Oates, Dr Edward Wilson, and seaman Edgar Evans. Then, seemingly on a whim, Scott added the name of Lt Birdie Bowers. It was a crazy decision. The tent would be overcrowded, a carefully worked-out routine would be thrown into chaos and the food and equipment taken for four men

Above: *Scott's party finds Amundsen's tent at the South Pole. Inside was a letter addressed to Scott, who wrote in his log: 'Great God, this is an awful place.'*

'I HAD THE SAME FEELING … AS A LITTLE BOY ON THE NIGHT BEFORE CHRISTMAS EVE – AN INTENSE EXPECTATION OF WHAT WAS GOING TO HAPPEN.'

would now have to extend to five. Moreover, Bowers had left his skis at the bottom of the Beardmore Glacier. He would have to trudge while the others slid along.

They set out in more blizzards, which reduced the pace to just ten miles a day. At first Scott was upbeat, writing in his diary: 'It is wonderful to see that two long marches will land us at the Pole ... it ought to be a certain thing now and the only appalling possibility is the sight of the Norwegian flag forestalling ours.'

THE DEATH OF HOPE

But after 15 January his writings became gloomier. He noted: 'We started off in high spirits in the afternoon feeling that tomorrow would see us at our destination. About the second hour of that march Bowers' sharp eyes detected what he thought was a cairn ... half an hour later he detected a black speck. We marched on and found that it was a black flag tied to a sledge bearer; nearby the remains of a camp ... this told us the whole story. The Norwegians have forestalled us and are first at the Pole. It is a terrible disappointment for me and I am very sorry for my loyal companions.'

Scott at last reached his goal on 18 January 1912. He found Amundsen's tent and a letter addressed to himself. Tired and devoid of morale, the British made camp and contemplated their shattered dreams. Scott himself wrote: 'Great God, this is an awful place. Now for the run home and a desperate struggle. I wonder if we can do it.' Maybe he already realized that time had run out. The bitter Antarctic winter would soon be closing in.

On 25 January his log states: 'Only 89 miles to the next depot but it is time we cleared off this plateau ... Oates suffers from a very cold foot; Evans' fingers and

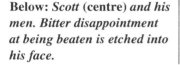

Below: *Scott* (centre) *and his men. Bitter disappointment at being beaten is etched into his face.*

nose are in a bad state and tonight Wilson is suffering tortures from his eyes … I fear a succession of blizzards at this time of year … not only stopping our marches but the cold, damp air takes it out of us.' As he wrote these words Amundsen was celebrating his own return to the Bay of Whales base camp. He'd gone there and back in 99 days – a journey of 1,860 miles across the most treacherous land in the world.

Despite their hardship, Scott's men found time to pursue their scientific objectives. On 7 February they arrived at the head of the Beardmore Glacier and immediately set about chipping off some of the rocks laid bare by the biting winds. They collected 35 lb before heading down to their base.

Now the problems began stacking up. First, they got lost and wasted vital rations trying to re-establish their route. Each man was down to his last meal when they stumbled upon the food depot they had been so desperately seeking. Then Edgar Evans fell and got himself concussed. He appeared dazed and rambling and, as Scott wrote, was 'absolutely changed from his normal self-reliant self'.

Later on, in the middle of a march, Evans dropped to his knees, uncovered hands bearing the ravages of frostbite, clothes dishevelled and 'a wild look in his eyes'. He died the same night. The survivors still had 430 miles to cover.

Captain Oates was the next to go. He no longer had the strength for sledge-hauling and could barely keep up because of his frostbitten feet. On 15 March he pleaded with the others to leave him behind so that they could improve their own chances. All three refused point-blank. But the following day a blizzard again swept in and the men were confined to their tent. In what was to become one of the most famous quotes in the history of exploration, the heroic Oates told his companions: 'I am going out and I may be some time'. He shuffled out into the driving snow where, somewhere, his body still lies.

Then came another setback. Oil had somehow managed to evaporate from the storage cans, which meant that the prospect of freezing to death became a distinct possibility. Two days after Oates vanished Scott, by now almost certainly in an exhausted mental state, wrote: 'We have the last half-fill of oil in our primus and a very small quantity of spirit – this alone between us and …'

On 21 March, while just 11 miles from their final supply depot, another blizzard confined them to their tent. Scott recorded: 'Had we lived, I should have had a tale to tell of the hardihood, endurance and courage of my companions that would have stirred the heart of every Englishman. These rough notes and our dead bodies must tell the tale but surely, surely, a great rich country such as ours will see that those who are dependent on us are properly provided for.'

THE GALLANT OATES TRIED TO SAVE HIS COMPANIONS BY LEAVING THE TENT AND STAGGERING TO HIS DEATH IN THE ICY BLIZZARD.

At about the same time, Scott penned a letter to Wilson's wife. It read: 'If this letter reaches you, Bill and I will have gone out together. We are very near it now and I should like you to know how splendid he was at the end – everlastingly cheerful and ready to sacrifice himself for others, never a word of blame to me for leading him into this mess.

'I can do no more to comfort you than to tell you that he died as he lived, a brave, true man – the best of comrades and the staunchest of friends. My whole heart goes out to you in pity. Yours, R. Scott'

Then, at the end of March, came the final entry in the journal. 'Every day now we have been ready to start for our depot eleven miles away, but outside the door of the tent it remains a scene of whirling drift. I do not think we can hope for any better

Above: *Captain Oates' supreme sacrifice. He dragged himself out into the teeth of a snowstorm, hardly able to stand on his frostbitten feet. His final words to his friends have become enshrined in the history of exploration.*

Above: *Scott's grave in the ice that claimed his life.*

things now. We shall stick it out to the end but we are getting weaker of course and the end cannot be far. R. Scott. For God's sake look after our people.'

The bodies were not found for eight months. Wilson and Bowers had their sleeping bags closed, Scott's was open – one arm thrown across Wilson. Reports of the scene plunged the whole of Britain into mourning.

On two counts the expedition had been truly a spectacular failure. It had failed to reach the Pole first and five of its members had met their deaths in the most appalling circumstances.

But out of that failure came a breath of triumph. For all his faults, occasional muddle-headedness and temper tantrums, Robert Scott elevated the qualities of courage and determination to heights rarely seen. He died a hero. Few men have matched him.

RUDOLPH HESS
A blunder of a peace mission

Rudolph Hess's desperate peace mission seemed too incredible to be true and the British politicians were wary. It was to be another 30 years before facts emerged that indicated that the real story might be even more amazing.

HE WAS BESOTTED BY HITLER AND DESCRIBED HIM AS 'FULL OF RARE DECENCY, FULL OF HEARTFELT GOODNESS …'

Hitler never wanted to go to war with Chamberlain or Churchill. Despite his curt treatment of Britain's premiers, it is often recounted how he saw Russia as his main target, to provide an ample empire for the German race. The Führer would have preferred Britain as an ally rather than an enemy in his fight against the bogey of Bolshevism.

With this in mind, and with astonishing gall, his right-hand man Rudolph Hess decided to seek peace with Britain. He probably believed he had every chance of succeeding too. With the island fortress taking a heavy battering and thought to be staring into the jaws of defeat, he was guessing that the beleaguered British politicians would seize the chance an honourable end to hostilities.

In a covert expedition, Hess set off for enemy soil with the intention of seeing a Scottish duke he had previously met. This nobleman, he was confident, would introduce him to King George VI whom he felt sure shared the same repulsion as Hess himself suffered at the wholesale loss of life in the conflict.

But for a man of renowned intellect his decision was a blunder of enormous proportions. No one knows if he discussed the mad peace plan with Hitler. No one knows if he had lost his mind thanks to the grim reality of a world at war. In fact, no one even knows whether the real Rudolph Hess was incarcerated as a war criminal for 46 years in Spandau Prison, Berlin. What is sure, however, is that the night flight from Germany put an end to his glittering career and, in real terms, his life.

Walter Rudolph Richard Hess was born in Egypt on 26 April 1894, the son of a young German merchant forging a successful business in Alexandria. His abiding memories of the era spent in Egypt were of expeditions with his mother to witness nature in action in the desert beneath a scorching sun or by night under a star-lit canopy.

By 1908 he had left Africa for college at Godesberg on the Rhine and later went to a French-speaking school in Switzerland. He was being tutored in accounts and business studies in preparation for taking on his father's import and export business, not a role he relished.

ACE PILOT

So when World War 1 broke out in 1914 he volunteered to serve in the infantry, seeing action in some of the bloodiest and foulest of killing fields, including the Somme and Verdun. Despite two injuries, he fought on. It wasn't until a bullet pierced his left lung, almost killing him, that he was discharged and returned to friendly territory for convalescence. But it wasn't the end of his war. He emerged again as a fighter pilot a month before the war ended, and there was more fighting to be done in the chaos that consumed Germany after 1918. During this turbulent time he met the father-figure he yearned for, Dr Karl Haushofer, an academic who shared his views on politics and racial purity.

In 1920 he enrolled at university to study history and economics and that same year he first met and fell under the spell of Adolf Hitler. Struck by his tremendous oratory, Hess enrolled in the newly formed National Socialist Party on 1 July as member number 16.

In those early days Hess described Hitler as ' … a character full of rare decency, full of heartfelt goodness, religious and a good Catholic. He has only one aim and for this he sacrifices himself quite unselfishly.'

Hess himself was a rather dour individual not given to laughter or joking. He did not smoke or drink and socialized only to broaden his mind by intense debate with other earnest young men looking for a new resurgence for their beloved homeland. He was certainly gullible and more than a little naïve, but stoically loyal.

When Hitler organized his uprising or *Putsch* in November 1923, Hess was at his side. They were consequently jailed for their insurrection and spent countless hours together during the 14 months they spent in a prison cell, exchanging ideas and discussing policies. Undoubtedly, Hess had a considerable input in Hitler's famous tome *Mein Kampf,* written at this time.

So the bond between Hitler and Hess was strengthening. In Hitler's subsequent climb to total power, Hess was in his shadow, working wholeheartedly for Nazism. There seemed a genuine affection between the two, shown when Hitler banned Hess from flying because he considered some of the stunts pulled off by the ace pilot too risky.

But Hess did have a distaste for wanton violence and mayhem even then. The brutality which emerged in bursts from Hitler, the leader he adored, were upsetting to him, to say the least. Most notable was the bloody purge Hitler carried out among his followers in the thirties after which Hess had to find words of explanation and comfort for distraught mothers and widows.

Hess had married his secretary Ilse Prohl but with little enthusiasm. Subsequently historians have questioned his sexuality, wondering whether or not he was gay. Some go as far as to list Albrecht Haushofer, son of the influential professor, the Duke of Hamilton and Hitler himself as Hess's partners.

It does appear the planned violent onslaught against Britain was causing Hess some anxiety. Previous peace offers to the British had fallen on deaf ears. In desperation, Hess turned to his old friend and confidant Haushofer who not only sympathized but passed on the name of a family friend in Lisbon, a Mrs Violet Roberts, who perhaps could help as an intermediary.

News that London was being pounded by the Luftwaffe and the sight of Berlin in flames convinced Hess that peace was preferable at any price. He authorized the letter to be sent to Lisbon, apparently unaware or uncaring that it might be intercepted by the British Secret Service, which it duly was.

When no reply came from Britain he sent his own letter, to which there was also no response. German morale was soaring so he knew any actions he took were unlikely to dent it. Also, he felt the Führer could easily extricate himself from the escapade which he admitted had little chance of success.

He then secured himself a plane from his flier friend Professor Willi Messerschmitt, ensuring it had sufficient capability to get him to Britain. It took some months of preparation and several abortive missions before the flight from which there would be no turning back took place. He wrote two letters to Hitler, several to his family and one to Heinrich Himmler, an adversary rather than comrade, protesting the innocence of all his men. In fact, only a couple of people did know about his plan, all of them among his staff. While others may have had their suspicions, Professor Haushofer, the man in whom he had confided many of his ambitions and woes during the previous 20 years, said he was ignorant of the peace bid. His wife Ilse, at home in bed because of illness on the day of his departure, knew nothing of his aims.

Above: Hess with Hitler and others of the Nazi hierarchy. He was a valued confidante and advisor to the Führer, which made him an object of envy among other leading Nazis.

Above: *Before the outbreak of World War 2, Hess helps Hitler to rally support.*

THE BLAZING PLANE CRASHED IN THE FIELD AND A LONE PARACHUTIST DRIFTED, BILLOWING DOWN TO EARTH IN THE MOONLIGHT.

TAKE-OFF

On 10 May 1941 the day dawned bright and sunny but the cloud cover Hess needed to breach Scotland's coast in safety was forecast and appeared. At last, this was the day he had waited for. Nobody thought twice about the Deputy Führer entering Augsberg airfield on an apparently workaday mission. After watching the tanks being filled and checking the guns were empty, Hess dropped into the cockpit and prepared for take-off. By 5.45 pm he was airborne, leaving Nazi Germany behind him for ever.

The circumstances of his arrival in Scotland are well documented. Shortly before 11 pm, a ploughman by the name of David McLean, of Floor's Farm, Eaglesham, near Glasgow, was deafened by a roar which shook his whole house. He rushed outside to see a plane crashed and blazing in a field and a lone parachutist billowing down to Earth in the moonlight.

At a distance, McLean called: 'Who are you? Are you German?' The reply stunned him. 'Yes, I am German. My name is Hauptmann Alfred Horn. I want to go to Dungavel House. I have an important message for the Duke of Hamilton.'

The plane had already been detected by radar as it crossed the Scottish coast. Either it was not intercepted or the weaponry used to shoot it down was defeated by the speed of the lone Messerschmitt. Royal Observer Corps staff were puzzled as to why a short range single German plane was traversing enemy airspace.

Nearby, the local home guard had also witnessed the spectacular descent of the aircraft and helped to take the pilot prisoner. Hess was unlikely to make an escape. He had badly sprained his ankle with his bumpy landing and was ensconced in McLean's comfy cottage when reinforcements arrived.

With an ancient revolver prodding his back, they left the farm for the home guard headquarters, a scout hut in Giffnock, a Glaswegian suburb. It took several hours for the wheels to grind into action. An interpreter, the Polish consul, was found. Two Royal Observer Corps officers arrived, one of whom immediately suspected the uninvited guest was Hess.

Maintaining his name was Horn and even brandishing an envelope bearing the name in a bid to convince his captors of the bogus identity, Hess asked once again to see the Duke of Hamilton.

A MISSION OF HUMANITY

Bizarrely, there was no response that night from RAF Turnhouse, under the command of the Duke of Hamilton, despite requests from the ROC men. It wasn't until 10 am the following day that the Duke turned up to interview the mystery prisoner. Hess requested a private audience with Hamilton during which he confessed for the first time that he was really Rudolph Hess and outlined the purpose of his flight. He was on a 'mission of humanity', he told Hamilton. 'The fact that I as a Reichsminister have come to this country in person is proof of my sincerity and Germany's willingness for peace.' Further, he wanted a guarantee to be able to return to Germany, whether or not his mission succeeded.

Churchill was duly briefed about the airman still known as Horn, by now held in a military hospital in Buchanan Castle at Drymen, four miles outside Glasgow.

The cigar-sucking statesman was wary. Although Hamilton and the foreign secretary Anthony Eden professed the prisoner bore a striking resemblance to Hess whom they had both met before the war, the Duke was doubtful about the story. With a string of military mishaps behind him in the opening rounds of the war, could he really be lucky enough to capture a high-ranking Nazi with such ease? Of course, the possibility of an impostor claiming to be Hess was examined, but Churchill and his colleagues were at a loss to know what game Hitler was playing, with such odd tactics. They were still pondering when German radio broadcast that Hess had gone missing in a disturbed mental state.

Later the Nazi propaganda machine churned out bulletins describing how Hess, an angel of peace, had been lured into an evil British trap. It appeared the Germans, too, were having difficulty explaining away the bizarre actions of Hess. Hitler, by all accounts, was stunned at the letter he received from Hess detailing his plans, and decided the fate of his old friend was held in the stars. Hess had promised he would not reveal the German plan to invade Russia in only a few weeks' time. Opening war on another front was a policy Hess believed to be madness, which was partly why he sought an accord with Britain. In the rambling explanation of his actions, Hess pointed out the Führer could simply deem his former deputy gone mad if any tricky questions arose. In turn, Hitler ordered that Hess be shot should he ever appear on German soil again.

Perhaps because the British military minds were so amazed at the German aviator's actions, they did not cash in on the capture of Hess in terms of morale-boosting publicity. They probably believed that the public, like themselves, would be unable to comprehend what had happened. Instead, they chose a whispering campaign designed to reach Germany only, alluding to Hess quitting Germany because he had lost confidence in the leadership and knew the war would be won by the British.

Hess was denied a piece of his aircraft as a memento, but allowed books, one of them being *Three Men in a Boat* by Jerome

Below: *Hess speaking publicly in 1937. He fervently believed in the Nazi policies of racial purity and national expansion, but disliked the party's lust for violence.*

K. Jerome. Later he requested a gun, probably planning to shoot himself, but was told the British government were short of guns at that time.

Lord Simon, the Lord Chancellor, posed as a psychiatrist in an interview with Hess in 1941. He reported that Hess had certainly come on the mission under his own steam and that Hitler knew nothing of the venture. He came to the conclusion, like many others, that Hess realized his own position in the hierarchy was being undermined despite unswerving, dog-like loyalty to his leader. It was his intention to pull off a coup with a negotiated peace that would ensure his position beside the Führer thereafter.

He also noted some worrying garbled comments from Hess which would have cast doubt on his sanity. Hess was convinced his food was being poisoned and that assassins lurked, waiting to finish him off. The British authorities were reluctant to declare Hess, codenamed Jonathan, insane because if they had there would have been various difficulties in holding

him as a prisoner. He would most likely have been sent back to Germany under the rules of the Geneva Convention.

Hess was possibly expecting a grander reception and certainly better living quarters after his arrival in Britain, but the barbed wire and sentries which guarded him were in part to protect him from revenge plots. There was evidence that Polish servicemen planned to kidnap him and at the very least rough him up in retribution for the treatment their country had suffered at German hands.

He tried to commit suicide at least once during the war – he leaped over a stairwell at Mytchett Place, Surrey, where he was being held. The injuries he sustained were not life threatening. There were bouts of amnesia in which Hess claimed he could not answer any questions about himself.

JUDGEMENT AT NUREMBERG

When the war ended it was decided he was capable of standing trial at Nuremberg

Below: The *Duke of Windsor, exiled from Britain after the abdication scandal, was friendly with the Führer and visited Germany in 1937 to inspect Nazi troops.*

alongside other notorious war criminals. At this time he set out his reasoning more concisely than ever before.

'The basis of my policy … must be an understanding with England. Even today, I have not yet given up this hope. I consider this war in which for a second time within a generation the people of a noble race are decimating each other and destroying their very substance as a terrible tragedy.

'The decision to go [from Germany] was the hardest I have ever made in my life. It was rendered easier, however, when I visualized the endless rows of coffins, both in Germany and in England, with mothers in dire distress following behind. I am convinced that mothers on both sides of the Channel will have understood my action.'

Along with Admiral Donitz, Admiral Raeder, Albert Speer and others, he was sentenced to life imprisonment at Spandau Prison in West Berlin. He was known as prisoner number 7. And here he spent year upon year in solitary confinement, held while other prisoners were allowed to go free. By 1967 he was the sole inmate in the complex, being guarded by a rota of British, American, French and Russian troops. It was the Russians who were most eager to see his imprisonment continue. Without Hess, they would have been banished from this legitimate foothold in West Berlin. Not only that, they were convinced he had helped draw up plans to obliterate Russia although it was claimed in London he knew nothing of Operation Barbarossa, Hitler's ill-fated invasion of the USSR.

Unaccountably, it was 23 years before Hess agreed to see his wife Ilse and son Wolf. By August 1987 the frail 93-year-old held in Spandau was ready to die. He committed suicide by strangling himself on the flex of a lamp. The bleak prison building was demolished soon afterwards but the controversy about Hess raged on.

Hess could have been the lone diplomat he always claimed, seeking to make peace, his brain becoming addled through pressure first exerted at home in Germany and later under interrogation.

There is also the suggestion that Hess was merely an expedient pawn, that peace negotiations were well under way and Hess was assigned for the most prominent and dangerous of roles by Hitler, to secure an

armistice. For whatever reason, the British side chose to abort the peace mission, if only to satisfy the masses who had pulled together for victory in a way no one imagined possible.

It is known Hess talked to the Duke of Windsor about an end to hostilities with Britain. The misguided Duke, who abdicated the throne for the love of American divorcee Wallis Simpson, was probably convinced the British would capitulate rather than face bloodshed. Any successfully negotiated peace would perhaps have removed King George VI from the throne and reinstated the banished Duke. The intervention of the incumbent King would have possibly been enough to scupper peace plans which certainly some members of the aristocracy favoured.

IMPOSTOR!

Then there is the storm caused by Dr Hugh Thomas, a consultant in Berlin's British Military Hospital, who became convinced the Hess held behind bars was an

Above: *Churchill in characteristic pose. He was perplexed by the bizarre actions of Hess and couldn't understand why the high-ranking German had taken flight from Germany.*

'I AM CONVINCED THAT MOTHERS ON BOTH SIDES OF THE CHANNEL WILL HAVE UNDERSTOOD MY ACTION.'

impersonator. He drew his amazing conclusions after witnessing the naked body of the ageing prisoner. In 1973 he was allowed to give Hess a complete medical check-up. The Russians were insistent that no comfort was shown to prisoner number 7. Their hardened attitude nearly resulted in the death of Hess in 1969 when they failed to call in help for several days after a duodenal ulcer perforated. On humanitarian grounds, Dr Thomas was anxious to see Hess accorded decent treatment. His discovery was electrifying.

History recorded how Hess as a young man had sustained a serious lung injury among others, but his body revealed no sign of a scar. On a subsequent examination, Dr Thomas asked: 'What happened to your war wounds?' According to the doctor, Hess blanched, trembled and uttered: 'Too late, too late.'

Convinced the real Hess was not the man who had been held for all these years by the Allies, Dr Thomas looked again at the flight from Germany. The plane used could not have covered the distance between Germany and Scotland without extra fuel tanks, yet a photograph taken by Hess's adjutant revealed no fuel tanks fixed to the wings of the aircraft.

There was the mystery of why he refused to see his wife and son – perhaps for fear of being revealed as an impostor. There were also lapses in his memory which no one could account for, when he failed to recognize people the real Hess had known well. The fastidious vegetarian Hess was known to be had also been replaced by a man greedy for food who would scoff meat, fish and anything else that came his way in a sloppy, unappealing manner.

Dr Thomas's theory is that Hess died in Germany before making his flight. News that he planned a hare-brained ploy for peace filtered through to other aspiring Nazi commanders – with up to five failed attempts at making the flight, it would not be surprising. Goering is known to have hated Hess and the intimate relationship he had with Hitler. Himmler, head of the SS, yearned to replace Hitler at the top. Both wanted Hess out of the way, but killing him would have offended his all-powerful long-time friend.

So they murdered the real Hess but had to make sure that a ringer arrived in Britain in his place to appease Hitler. Why would anyone take on such a thankless role? Many reluctant volunteers enlisted in fear of what might happen to their families if they wavered. After weeks or months of brainwashing, a lookalike might have been genuinely confused about fact and fantasy. He might accurately have guessed that any protestations at the Nuremberg trials would not have been believed.

There is even a theory that James Bond creator Ian Fleming entered into a ritual with satanist Aleister Crowley to lure Hess to Britain after the powerful deputy had been identified as a weak link in the chain of power. A biographer of Fleming says that in 1941 in Ashdown Forest, Sussex, Fleming joined Crowley and his son Amando in flowing robes chanting a spell which would woo Hess to British shores.

Official papers, however, concur with the notion that Hess worked alone and was indeed rather mentally disturbed at the time of his flight to Britain. Brigadier J. Rees, consultant psychiatrist from the army who tended Hess during his internment in Britain, wrote that he suffered from: 'periodic spells of depression and generalised nervousness ... he is suffering from insomnia and from attacks of abdominal discomfort'.

National archive material released in 1992 discounts the numerous conspiracy theories. No doubt is noted among the politicians of the day involved in the issue about the identity of the parachutist. Interviewers reported how he seemed resigned to his lonely future after deciding the mission for peace was his fate or destiny. Hess always denied Hitler had sent him. One government paper is being withheld for security reasons.

Whatever the truth, it is certain that when Hess hatched the plot to become unofficial emissary for peace, he was sealing his own miserable fate. Either he was killed in a hush-hush operation by his rivals in the Reich or he condemned himself to a life of bitter solitude lasting year upon interminable year, never to be shown mercy. While his prospects in Germany long term were perhaps less than shining, at least he would have escaped living in limbo and might have died with honour, something he would certainly have valued.

THE DISCOVERY WAS ELECTRIFYING – AND EXPLAINED WHY HESS HAD REFUSED TO SEE HIS WIFE AND SON FOR OVER 20 YEARS.